Contents
POTS, PANS & PROPHECIES

Acknowledgements

There are many people who have given of their talents and their time to whom I owe so much.

I want to thank Rhonda Holland for believing in each of you as well as the ministry of Women's Discipleship by pouring her heart out through the taught Word; Annette Alsobrooks at Ballew Graphics that designed our cover and book design; Chad Guyton and the 5:01 Studios team for their professional work on the teaching DVD; Michael McDonald, for flowing, editing/graphic design enhancement; Joel Barnes for pouring over the manuscript during the editing process; Crista Barnes for checking and double checking all scripture references; my husband, David, for his love and patience during this process; and a very special thanks to my assistant, Kristina Higgins, for her initial work with editing, video graphics placement and editing, and for keeping the office running smoothly during the whole process.

My prayer is that we will all be able to say, "Yes," to being a vessel that is clean, accessible, willing to hold the ingredients, and able to take the heat" so that we are vessels God can use for His mission.

—Lorna V. Gosnell
International Women's Discipleship Coordinator
2010-2017

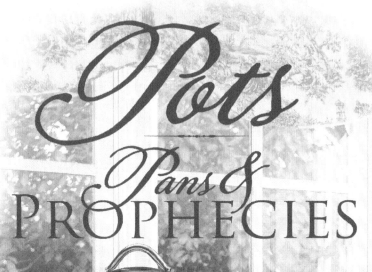

PROPHECIES

INTRODUCTION

POTS, PANS & PROPHECIES

by Rhonda K. Holland

Introduction

2 Timothy 2:20-21

Some of us love to cook, some of us love for others to cook for us, and some of us like to go out for a good meal. I think all of us fall into one or more of those categories at times!

Regardless of whether we are the chef or the recipient of the meal prepared, there are some things about cooking that we all have in common. We have to have vessels—pots and pans of some sort for our food to be prepared. There are also certain basic things that are required in order for those vessels to be used.

None of us would prepare a meal in a dirty pot or eat a meal that we knew was prepared in one. The pot or pan used would have to be clean—always! So first of all, the main thing in determining whether or not we use a pot or pan to prepare a dish would be that *it has to be clean!*

Secondly, the pot or pan *has to be accessible.* As the cook in my own kitchen, like you, there are some requirements that are just a given. Absolutely, the pot or pan must be clean before I would use it and I have got to be able to find it! Have you ever looked for a pot or pan and couldn't locate it? It may be one that you only use for certain events or special occasions, but if it is not accessible to you—you can't use it!

I have a huge pot that I only use when I have a large group or my extended family over. So I usually put it away until I know I am going to need it. One year, my husband had stored this favorite big stew pot of mine in a box with my Christmas decorations! His explanation to me was that it is because I only used it around the holidays. It made perfect sense to him, but if the pot was unavailable to me when I needed it, it was of no use—even if it was clean. I was just about to give up on using my favorite stew pot because I couldn't find it, when my husband came in and told me where he had put it. Therefore, before a pot or pan can be used—it has to be accessible to the chef.

Thirdly, the pot I use has to be the right size and texture to be able to handle and hold the ingredients I have for my recipe. The right pot *has to be able to hold the ingredients*. It is up to me as the cook to understand which pot or pan is the right vessel of choice for what I want to prepare. I choose based on what recipe I desire to complete, and I factor in the purpose for which the pot or pan was created as to whether it is right for this dish.

Also, the pot or pan *has to be seasoned and tempered in order to take the heat required* to prepare the dish. The right vessel *will be able to take the heat!* If a pot or pan is not able to take the heat or endure the required time in the oven for what I am preparing, I must choose another.

My choice in determining which pot or pan in my kitchen to use for a particular purpose doesn't

mean that another one not used at the time is any less important or needed than the other, it just means that I have to choose the right one to use according to its ability and according to what I want or need prepared at the time.

Now let's use our imaginations a little bit!

What if the pots and pans in your kitchen were alive, living beings, each with their own personality? What if they were the ones trying to decide when and for what they would be used and could argue and reason with you about your choices for their use? What if the pots thought they had to plan the meals and purchase the ingredients? If the pots and pans could decide, chances are they would never want a tasteless or bitter or sour ingredient placed in them. It is likely that they would choose only the sweet and tasteful ingredients for themselves!

But it's the chef who knows that sometimes the ingredients include the bitter, sour, and sometimes the seemingly tasteless ones to create the perfect recipe.

What if the pots and pans had to choose which among themselves would be used to go into the oven next? What if they could choose which would be used to prepare the main dish or the dessert? What if they could choose which one got to "sit this one out" and wait until the next meal? What if they were jealous or angry because you used one pot more than the others? If the pots and pans were in charge of the

kitchen, I can imagine that they would be sure to get credit for the delicious meals prepared. Imagine how you would feel if your husband, friend or family member walked up to the large pot on the stove and thanked it for the awesome bowl of chili you just served! What if someone walked over to the pan you just took from the oven and thanked it for the amazing and tasty casserole you just dished out for them?

No, in reality, even though they are essential for a meal to be completed, pots and pans are never given nor do they take the credit for what is prepared! The success of the dish always goes to the chef!

Real pots and pans in our kitchen never worry about what the vessel on the shelf beside it is created to accomplish. They don't become envious or jealous if one pot seems to be used more often or for "better" things. The choice of when and for what the pots and pans are to be used is solely the responsibility of the chef, never the vessels!

As the main chef for my family, (*no offense to real chefs—I know I am just a home cook!*) I plan and purchase the ingredients for the meal I want to prepare for them. I go to my favorite grocery store and take the time to choose carefully the items, buy them, take them to the car and place them from the cart to the back seat of my vehicle. I take them home and unload them from the car to the kitchen. Now I have taken my time and expense to go out and purchase

INTRODUCTION

and bring home what I need to prepare the meal. I've brought in all the required items to complete my delicious dishes. The ingredients are there in my kitchen–bought and paid for. However, *I still have to have my pots and pans* or I cannot prepare what I want for my family to benefit from and enjoy. I need more than just the right ingredients to accomplish my goal! *I must have vessels.*

> *I must have pots and pans that are:*
> *Clean, accessible, that can handle the*
> *ingredients, and are able to take the heat,*
> *or I am unable to accomplish my mission!*

In God's house there are many vessels with many purposes. We are those vessels!

> But in a great house there are not only vessels of gold and of silver, but also of wood and of earth; and some to honour, and some to dishonour. If a man therefore purge himself from these, he shall be a vessel unto honour, sanctified, and meet for the master's use, and prepared unto every good work (2 Tim. 2:20-21 KJV).

We are "living vessels" in God's house! And like our imaginary "living pots and pans" we just discussed, we do sometimes try to reason and even argue with the Master about His plans for us and our desire in our choice of service for Him.

We must remember that He has created each of us with a perfect plan in mind. The plan He has for you will be beneficial to you and to those around you. You will be blessed while being a blessing when His purpose is complete in you, *but first, before He can use you for His glory, you must be clean, accessible and able to take the heat. You also must trust Him with the ingredients and know that He is working a beautiful plan with an amazing result! You must purpose to never take the credit for what He accomplishes through you. All glory goes to Him!*

Just like the pots and pans in our kitchens, as vessels in the Father's house, we do not decide when or for what we are used. We are to trust Him to make those choices and believe Him for the end accomplishments He has promised when we yield ourselves to Him in service. *Complete trust requires us to lay aside our logic and reasoning. It is impossible to do that without a very real revelation of who God is!*

Throughout this study, we will also look at the importance of being a yielded vessel that meets the required qualifications for use by God. We will also discuss the necessity of keeping the true revelation of God before us as we walk in His plan and purpose. We will be reminded that *it is not a realization of our own strength, power, abilities, resources, and talents that we need or depend on, but rather a redemptive revelation of Him. We will also realize when those times arise that there is a lack of our own strength, power, abilities, resources or talents it will not inhibit us from doing God's will when we keep true revelation of who God is before us.*

When Jesus died on the cross, He provided the atonement for our sins. His precious blood redeems and cleanses us when we accept and acknowledge Him as our Savior. Through His obedience to His Father's will, Jesus purchased all the "ingredients" needed to create in us what He desires to accomplish for us and through us. We have the wonderful Holy Spirit as our Teacher and Guide and He will empower us and lead us as we walk as obedient vessels!

A Point to Ponder: When Jesus cried out on the cross, "It is finished!" He didn't mean His life had ended—He meant the plan was accomplished. Praise His Name! He came and paid a high price for our sins and our redemption, and if I can trust Him with my eternity, I can surely trust Him for today. Rest is His declaration from Calvary. It is finished! Rejoice because what He accomplished cannot be undone.

Yet still, even with all the ingredients and power from God available to accomplish His purpose, God needs clean, yielded, and accessible vessels that are willing and able to take the heat. He desires to use vessels of honor that will never take the credit for what He accomplishes through them. He desires to use those who will lay aside their own agendas and allow Him to use them as He sees fit. He wants us to all work with one another, each walking according to our created purpose so that together we can accomplish greater things for Him.

In *Pots, Pans & Prophecies*, we will study together the journey of the yielded vessel. We will discuss the battles we face on the road to the promise. We will purpose in our hearts to become that willing, consistent, and dependable vessel God can use to further His Kingdom. We will share together as we learn of the amazing joy and liberty that comes from God as we live a life of obedience before Him. We will see through the Word of God the incredible peace and assurance that results in the life of one that is submitted to God's plan.

Mary, the mother of Jesus, is a wonderful example in the Word of God of one who was clean, accessible, able, and willing to endure the heat of the battles she faced in order to allow God's perfect will to be completed in her vessel.

We will journey together from the beginning of Mary's recorded story according to the Gospel of Luke. We will start with the proclamation of the promise given to her and conclude with the performance of that promise.

As we begin this study together, ask God to help you, like Mary, to completely surrender to His perfect will and plan for your life. As we reflect together on the life of Mary, you will be assured that the fulfillment of His perfect plan concerning you will be worth the sometimes-painful process it takes to get there. Like Mary's story, your obedience will

Dear God:

bring great joy to your life and to the Body of Christ, and no matter the obstacles or battles fought in the process to His promise, He will be with you every step of the journey as you walk in obedience to Him. *His presence ensures victory!*

Plan to take the time and journal as you go through this study. Journaling will help you express your heart and will also help you to retain important thoughts that the Lord will give you as you spend time in the Word.

Please take a moment and pray the following prayer of commitment before you begin the study of *Pots, Pans & Prophecies*.

Lord, as I begin this study I renew my commitment to give my life completely to You and Your will and plan. I want to live my life as a vessel of Your grace, cleansed by Your blood, accessible to Your plan, trusting You with the ingredients I'm dealt, whether sweet or bitter. I want to be strong and endure the heat that is sometimes required to bring forth what You have planned for me. I will find rest in my revelation

of who You are to me. Your constant presence will comfort me when the journey is difficult. I plan to find joy in each day I have been given by continually abiding in Your Word. Your peace will accompany me as I journey in this life because I am assured You will never leave me or forsake me. I will take refuge in You when the storms of life are raging and my confidence in You will be greater than the winds that are blowing. I will praise You daily, believing that what You have planned for my life is greater than I ever imagined. I will also rejoice knowing my eternal rewards for walking in obedience to You in this life are beyond my greatest expectations!

INTRODUCTION

Week One

POWER TRUTH

Week One
POWER TRUTH
Proclamation of the Promise

We will begin with the journey of Mary as recorded in Luke.

Mary is the perfect example of a yielded vessel of honor. She submitted her life to God's plan and purpose.

We should follow Mary's example and walk in obedience to God's plan. We must lay down our reasoning and walk in our revelation of God, completely assured that His plan for us is better than our own. *Revelation of God is a necessary "ingredient" in your vessel.*

Jesus came so that we might experience an abundant life. Purpose to surrender to Him knowing that your obedience will be rewarded.

Mary was accessible to the plan and will of God. In doing so, she was also available as a recipient of the promises and provisions of God for her life.

The thief comes only in order to steal and kill and destroy. I came that they may have *and* enjoy life, and have it in abundance (to the full, till it overflows) (John 10:10 AB).

Week One

PROCLAMATION OF THE PROMISE

Week One
PROCLAMATION OF THE PROMISE
From Gabriel to Mary
Luke 1:31-33

The purpose of this study is to help us to live our lives continually as willing vessels of honor for God. It is so important that we keep in mind that *God's plans for our life are much better than our own!* While complete and total surrender can seem almost overwhelming we must remember that our Heavenly Father knows us better than we know ourselves. His love for us is greater than we can comprehend and we can rest assured knowing His plan for us is good. Life lived according to His plan always ends well, even if we do have battles from the adversary along the way.

> *God never writes a sad ending for us!*
> *He intends for us to have abundant*
> *life through Him.*

Let's read these Scriptures to help us hold on to those thoughts as we begin this study:

> The thief comes only in order to steal and kill and destroy. I came that they may have *and* enjoy life, and have it in abundance (to the full, till it overflows) (John 10:10 AB).

Pots, Pans & PROPHECIES

For I know the plans I have for you," declares the Lord, "plans to prosper you and not to harm you, plans to give you hope and a future. Then you will call on me and come and pray to me, and I will listen to you. You will seek me and find me when you seek me with all your heart (Jer. 29:11-13 NIV).

From these two Scriptures alone, His Word comforts us. Jesus declares that He came that we may have abundant life through Him! Life that is full and overflowing because of His love for us is promised through Him. What a contrast these two Scriptures give us between the enemy's plot to steal, kill, and destroy us and Jesus' plan to give us a good and blessed life.

Jeremiah 29:11-13 shows and speaks of God's love for His people and His desire to give us a future and a hope. We are assured that when we call on Him, He will hear us.

With these verses alone as our assurance, we know we can trust God's plan for our life. As we begin this study, keep in mind that God has great things prepared for those who yield to Him and walk in faith.

Let's reflect on what we discussed in the introduction. Before a vessel can be used, it must first be clean. When we accept Jesus as Savior and repent of our sins, His blood washes us, cleansing us from the stains of the sins we committed. We are washed and purified by Him.

PROCLAMATION OF THE PROMISE

And such some of you were [once]. But you were washed clean (purified by a complete atonement for sin and made free from the guilt of sin), and you were consecrated (set apart, hallowed), and you were justified [pronounced righteous, by trusting] in the name of the Lord Jesus Christ and in the [Holy] Spirit of our God (1 Cor. 6:11 AB).

So, the first requirement is met for our vessel to be used! We are clean!

However, *before* salvation can come, there must first be a *redemptive revelation of God* presented. To know Jesus Christ is the most wonderful gift ever offered to mankind. The world is suffering on so many levels because it is lacking revelation of the truth about God. Many are walking in darkness because they haven't been given revelation knowledge of Him. Some are walking in sin because they choose to disregard the revelation they have been given, but those who are saved and redeemed are those who responded to that revelation and received it as truth.

Read and meditate on the truth of this familiar verse:

Where there is no vision [no redemptive revelation of God], the people perish; but he who keeps the law [of God, which includes that of man]—blessed (happy, fortunate, and enviable) is he (Prov. 29:18 AB).

This powerful truth is so apparent around us today! The people have no redemptive revelation of God and they are perishing because of it.

Revelation is required before you have a relationship with Jesus Christ! You must have a revelation of the truth of who He is before you can give your heart and life to Him. When revelation is given, it requires a response. Revelation of God will cause you to either run to Him or run from Him. It will cause to you embrace His plan for your life or resist it. Whether received or rejected—revelation will demand a response. In order to walk in complete victory and trust as you yield to God's will and plan, you must rely on revelation knowledge—not logic or facts. *God is never bound or limited to man's logic, facts or circumstances.* You must determine to keep that revelation truth in the forefront of your mind as you journey in this life. Truth always overrides the facts!

Revelation of God is a necessary "ingredient" in your vessel.

Revelation, when accepted, is the beginning of a relationship with God. *The more your relationship grows, the more revelation you have of Him. The more revelation you have of Him, the less you will depend on your own understanding and reasoning.* The more revelation acquired about Him, the less likely you are to pick up logic instead of relying on that revelation knowledge. The more revelation you

PROCLAMATION OF THE PROMISE

have of God, the less your reasoning becomes a threat to His purpose in your life.

Now, before you go further in this study, read and meditate on Luke 1:26-56. This passage of Scripture will be the main text and the story that we will refer to throughout this study.

Notice in *Luke 1:28*, Gabriel addresses Mary and tells her that she is highly favored of God and blessed among women. God was aware of Mary's pure and clean life. He was mindful of her committed love toward Him. He knew she was qualified to be the mother of His Son.

> And having come in, the angel said to her, "Rejoice, highly favored *one*, the Lord *is* with you; blessed *are* you among women!" (v. 28).

Mary was a chosen vessel of honor!

In *Luke 1:30*, Gabriel instructs Mary to not be afraid. He again reminds her that she has found favor with God. Let's read it together in the Amplified Version:

> And the angel said to her, Do not be afraid, Mary, for you have found grace (free, spontaneous, absolute favor and loving-kindness) with God (v. 30 AB).

Mary found grace and favor with God!

Now, let's read again the *Proclamation of the Promise* by Gabriel to Mary in *Luke 1:31-33*:

> And behold, you will conceive in your womb and bring forth a Son, and shall call His name Jesus. He will be great, and will be called the Son of the Highest; and the Lord God will give Him the throne of His father David. And He will reign over the house of Jacob forever, and of His kingdom there will be no end (vv.31-33).

After Gabriel proclaims God's promise to Mary, there is a beautiful conversation recorded between them in the next five verses in this passage (Luke 1:34-38). Read and pay close attention to every important detail of their conversation:

> Then Mary said to the angel, "How can this be, since I do not know a man?" And the angel answered and said to her, "*The* Holy Spirit will come upon you, and the power of the Highest will overshadow you; therefore, also, that Holy One who is to be born will be called the Son of God. Now indeed, Elizabeth your relative has also conceived a son in her old age; and this is now the sixth month for her who was called barren. For with God nothing will be impossible." Then Mary said, "Behold the maidservant of the Lord! Let it be to me according to your word." And the angel departed from her (vv.34-38).

PROCLAMATION OF THE PROMISE

Mary simply and understandably asked concerning what she had just heard, "How can this be?"

Gabriel answered her and explained, "The Holy Spirit will come upon you and the power of the Highest will overshadow you; therefore, also that Holy One who is to be born will be called the Son of God."

Next, he revealed to her the miracle of Elizabeth's conception of her own son! Mary knew her cousin Elizabeth was too old to conceive and this would also be a miracle from God. Finally, Gabriel assured her that with God all things are possible.

Mary made herself accessible with a simple reply. She said, "Behold the maidservant of the Lord! Let it be to me according to your word."

*Mary made herself accessible to the plan
and will of God.*

Read Romans 12:1-2. In Paul's writings, he reminds us that our act of presenting ourselves to God as a "living and holy sacrifice" is real worship. So many times we determine whether or not we worship God faithfully by our church attendance alone. Our consistent church attendance is so important, but it is not the sole measure of our worship. Constant encouragement from a caring fellowship of believers helps us remain faithful to God and increases our knowledge and revelation of Christ through the teaching of His Word. It is vital that we congregate and be committed to a local church body, but we

are to also commit to worship God by presenting ourselves, yielded to His plan and purpose on a daily basis. That is genuine worship.

We are also reminded in this passage that we are to resist being conformed or molded into a pattern of thinking and living like the world around us. We are to continually allow the Spirit of God to transform our thinking—our reasoning—based on our revelation of Jesus Christ.

> Therefore I urge you, brethren, by the mercies of God, to present your bodies a living and holy sacrifice, acceptable to God, *which* is your spiritual service of worship. And do not be conformed to this world, but be transformed by the renewing of your mind, so that you may prove what the will of God is, that which is good and acceptable and perfect (Rom. 12:1-2 NASB).

The word "accessible" is defined in part as, "*being able to be used, approached and influenced.*" It is imperative for us as believers who have been cleansed and made righteous by His sacrifice at Calvary to also be accessible by God. We must set aside our own agendas and yield to His perfect plan. We must be teachable and willing to be influenced by the Spirit of God in order to truly submit to His plan.

We must be accessible, available and willing to walk according to His purpose for us!

PROCLAMATION OF THE PROMISE

The proclamation of a powerful promise had been given to Mary. She had accepted God's will for her life and was now about to begin a powerful and amazing journey that would change the course of her life and all mankind forever. She did not present a long list of questions for Gabriel to answer and she did not lose herself in her own logic. Mary did not begin reasoning away the possibility of everything the angel had just shared and revealed to her. *Mary laid down her reasoning and picked up her revelation!* Then, when she had received the revelation, she was able to confidently reply, "Let it be to me according to your word."

As a believer in Jesus Christ, you are a vessel with a purpose and a destiny. To accomplish your purpose you, like Mary, must make yourself accessible to His plan. *Lay down your reasoning and receive your revelation of what God desires to do in you and through you*! Remember, God *needs* vessels in these last days that are clean, accessible and able to take the heat.

Will you lay aside your personal agenda and wants to listen and really hear from Him?

Why must I lay aside my reasoning and logic? Oftentimes, we look to our own understanding and our own talents and abilities when God gives us a task or we feel a call to follow Him in a certain area of ministry. Sometimes, we feel inadequate or unqualified for a list of reasons that are as unique and

individual as we are. This will cause us to begin to reason away the calling or lay down our commitment to serve because we are basing everything on ourselves or our own logic or facts and circumstances surrounding our lives.

Mary could have laid down the revelation of what she had been told by Gabriel if she had gone down the path of her own understanding and reasoning. She, no doubt, was a faithful follower of God and knew the law and writings of the prophets of old. This would have made her familiar with the prophecies concerning the coming Messiah. She knew what the prophets said about Him and the promise of His birth. Certainly, she would have had the knowledge that it was prophesied that the Messiah would be born in Bethlehem and here she was in Nazareth! That alone would have been cause for argument if she had stepped into her reasoning rather than revelation.

If Mary had stepped into reasoning, she would have begun imagining how all the details of the proclamation given her might unfold. This would lead to her feeling she had to plan it all out. She would begin thinking of how she would have to "help make it happen." She would have immediately started making plans for her move to Bethlehem. She would have written details of her well-scripted speech attempting to explain to Joseph all that had been told to her by Gabriel. It would have included how they would have to relocate in order to be at the right place at the right time when the Babe was to be born.

PROCLAMATION OF THE PROMISE

Before she had finalized her "to-do" list, she would have begun doubting the reality of what had just been proclaimed to her. The voice of her own thoughts in her mind would have immediately started to override the revelation of truth given by Gabriel.

When we get lost in our own reasoning we can feel overwhelmed and begin to feel that we have to fulfill the will of God in our own power and ability and make it happen ourselves. However, when we walk in our revelation of who He really is, we recognize He is completely capable of bringing to completion what He has promised! We don't have to work out the details. We just yield to His will and walk in revelation knowledge that our God is able to bring it to fulfillment.

Remember, the pots and pans in our kitchens don't have to do the planning and work out the details in order to get the results of a successful recipe. That is up to the chef!

In God's house, as His vessel, I don't have to plan it out or work out the details. I yield to the Creator and trust something beautiful will come through my willing vessel in His perfect timing.

I must simply walk in revelation and not my own reasoning and yield to His perfect plan!

You can be assured that when you yield yourself to His plan, the rewards of walking in obedience are greater than you can imagine. The joy of seeing others changed and strengthened through your obedience is such a powerful blessing. The rewards of your obedience are eternal for both you and the lives that

are touched through you as you listen and obey His commands.

Like the pots and pans in our kitchen, we are all different. We all have various talents and personalities. We are all unique and individual creations of our Father but regardless of our individual calling or talents, we all have one thing in common. *We are all to build the kingdom*! We are to share the gospel and lead others to Christ while encouraging other Christians in this journey with us.

There are gifts and callings that are as unique and different as those called to walk in them.

Read Romans 12:3-8. We are reminded in these Scriptures that we are to serve God with spiritual gifts. It is also crucial to note the very important instructions given in verse 3, that one is not to "think of *himself* more highly than he ought to think, but to think soberly, as God has dealt to each one a measure of faith."

This passage does not mean that we are to feel worthless or unimportant. Instead, it is teaching us that we should never feel more important, more deserving of salvation or favor from God based on our talents or gifts or calling. Our talents, gifts, and callings belong to God! He created us and gave them to us to benefit the entire body. We are all of equal worth in the eyes of God.

Remember in the introduction when we imagined our pots in the kitchen having the ability to pick and choose what they did and when they served. The pots and pans don't have that responsibility or option and

PROCLAMATION OF THE PROMISE

in God's house the vessels do not choose either. God gives the talent and the calling. *Therefore, we are never to take the credit or glory!* We use what He has given us to serve Him and for the benefit of the entire Body of Christ.

Let's look together at *Ephesians 4:11-16*:

And He Himself gave some *to be* apostles, some prophets, some evangelists, and some pastors and teachers, for the equipping of the saints for the work of ministry, for the edifying of the body of Christ, till we all come to the unity of the faith and of the knowledge of the Son of God, to a perfect man, to the measure of the stature of the fullness of Christ; that we should no longer be children, tossed to and fro and carried about with every wind of doctrine, by the trickery of men, in the cunning craftiness of deceitful plotting, but, speaking the truth in love, may grow up in all things into Him who is the head—Christ—from whom the whole body, joined and knit together by what every joint supplies, according to the effective working by which every part does its share, causes growth of the body for the edifying of itself in love (vv.11-16).

In this passage of Scripture, we see the list of the fivefold ministry of the Church. List the five gifts from Christ recorded in verse 11, and then in your

own words write down the purpose of these gifts as explained in these verses:

_____

_____

_____

_____

_____

_____

_____

_____

_____

_____

We are to use the gifts of the apostle, prophet, evangelist, pastor, and teacher for the equipping of the saints for the continued work of the ministry. We are to edify each other in the body of Christ and work to have unity in our faith. We are to use these gifts to *increase our revelation knowledge of Jesus Christ and to establish us in sound doctrine.*

These gifts will strengthen us in our walk in truth so that we will not be "tossed to and fro and carried about with every wind of doctrine" that is now so prevalent in these last days.

Now, turn to 1 Corinthians 12:4-12 and read this passage. This powerful passage reminds us of the diversities of gifts while also reminding us that we are to work in unity as one body.

As we read in *Luke 1:38*, Mary accepted God's will for her life and immediately set her mind to walk in His purpose for her. Perhaps God is calling you

PROCLAMATION OF THE PROMISE

into a life of full-time ministry. Maybe you feel the call to teach or to preach the gospel. Possibly, you have felt a pull to a foreign land to share the Word as a missionary. You may feel God calling you to share a ministry responsibility with your spouse. Whatever God is calling you to do, be assured He has already equipped you to be able to fulfill the responsibilities and duties of that call!

Not everyone is called to a pulpit ministry. Not all are called to teach or preach to a congregation in a church or classroom, but all of us are called to walk in obedience to the Word and to share the truth of Jesus with our family, friends,, and those we work with and live around. We are to live a life that exemplifies Christ to all we meet.

Never underestimate the power or importance of the ministry God has entrusted to you in this life. As a mother, I have felt that my most important ministry role in life has been to instill truth into our sons and live a life pleasing to God before them.

More often than not, you have many roles in ministry. Perhaps you are the only Christian in your family or maybe you are a sibling to an unsaved brother or sister. Your example is constantly before them. You may have an unsaved spouse and you desire to draw them into the Family of God. You are a minister of Christ, teaching and reaching out in love with your actions, words, and deeds to your own family members. What a wonderful vessel of honor you are in service to God when you reach out to those you love the most!

God has chosen you to let your light shine in darkness everywhere you go—where you work or attend school or in your neighborhood. *Ministry opportunities are all around us*! God needs yielded vessels to obey Him in these last days and to reach the lost for Him.

It is so important that we yield ourselves to His plan for the benefit of the Kingdom in these perilous times but it is also a wonderful truth that when we yield to His plan we also open ourselves to receive His promises as declared in the Word. *When Mary submitted her life to God's will, she opened the door to receive the promises that come as a result of obedience.*

> *Mary was accessible to the plan and will of God and in doing so, she was also available as a recipient of the promises and provisions of God for her life!*

The sinner does not understand the contentment in the life of a committed Christian. The enemy would have them look at us as if we are in bondage and cannot enjoy the life the world offers. What they do not see is that we are set free from the sins that once entangled us. We have liberty and enjoy genuine freedom through Christ. When we walk in obedience to our Father, we choose life and not death; blessings and not curses. Like Mary, we become heirs to His promises and provisions.

PROCLAMATION OF THE PROMISE

Read Deuteronomy 28:2-14. Write some of the promises recorded in this powerful passage:

_____
_____
_____
_____
_____
_____
_____
_____
_____
_____
_____
_____
_____
_____
_____
_____

The Word of God is full of promises and prophecies for the believer! Have you been holding on to a promise that has been proclaimed in your life? Are you holding tightly to a passage of promise in the Word that has given you hope or strength for a battle you are fighting?

Write down a promise or a passage of Scripture that you are trusting God to fulfill in your life:

_____
_____
_____

_____

_____

_____

God's Word is eternal and His promises
are true!

The proclamation of a promise—The Promise —was given to Mary, but, it was contingent on her willingness to yield to God's plan and walk in obedience to Him. God would not have forced His will on Mary had she not been willing to accept His plan. He will not force His will on you for your life either. *The choice is yours*! You can enjoy the life of obedience to God and reap wonderful rewards in this life and in the life to come. Those who choose to ignore God's will often struggle daily with wrong choices and the regrets that come with them. We must choose to obey and walk according to His purpose. God's plan for you is perfect! It comes with great benefits. *If Mary had not submitted to His will, she would not have obtained the promises that accompanied the plan for her life.* But she did accept His will for her life and she embarked on a powerful and amazing journey that we still read, teach, preach, and celebrate today—and we will—*for all eternity!*

Remember, Mary did not begin reasoning away the possibility of the promise and everything the angel had just shared and revealed to her. *She laid down her reasoning and picked up her revelation!* We must do the same.

PROCLAMATION OF THE PROMISE

A Point to Ponder: Jesus is the Word and He willingly became flesh to live among us. (John 1:14) Mary carried the literal Word of God within her. As believers, we carry the Word hidden in our hearts. When it remains there and takes root, and our faith and obedience cause it to grow, something wonderful will be birthed from us to benefit the Kingdom of God!

When you have a promise proclaimed to you through the preached or printed Word of God and it quickens your heart and you reach out in faith to claim it, the enemy always comes immediately and tries to steal it away from you. He does not want it to take root in your heart and come forth and produce results. He tries to snatch away the seed before it is planted deep in your spirit. He does not want your life to benefit the Kingdom of God. *He wants to abort the seed of promise in you!* Satan's battleground is in our mind and he comes and tries to give us suggestions and reasoning that will diminish the power and promises of God in hopes of destroying your faith.

Read 2 Corinthians 10:3-6 and write down what it instructs us to do with the thoughts that come from the enemy.

For though we walk in the flesh, we do not war according to the flesh. For the weapons of our warfare *are* not carnal but mighty in God for pulling down strongholds, casting down arguments and every high thing that exalts

itself against the knowledge of God, bringing every thought into captivity to the obedience of Christ, and being ready to punish all disobedience when your obedience is fulfilled (vv. 10:3-6).

_____
_____
_____
_____
_____
_____
_____
_____
_____
_____

We are instructed to cast down every argument, thought, and reasoning that exalts itself against the knowledge of God. The thoughts that refute what God has said, the arguments in your mind that make you doubt His power working in you and for you, the suggestions that make you wonder if you deserve what God has promised you, the "logical reasoning" that says it is just impossible—all these thoughts are exalting themselves against the revelation you have been given. We are to bring those very thoughts into captivity and not allow them to run freely in our minds. If we do not bring them into captivity, our reasoning will cause us to get lost in our logic and we will begin to doubt the promise that has been proclaimed to us. When we receive that doubt, our revelation begins to fade and if we continue, we

PROCLAMATION OF THE PROMISE

allow the enemy to build a stronghold in our mind and sadly, we then *pick up our reasoning and lay down our revelation.*

Remember, Our God doesn't operate in logic.
He is never bound by facts or opinions.
He has proclaimed promises to you through
His Word. Hold on to them and declare His
truth over your life!

As Mary began this journey, trust was essential. Trust is necessary to walk out the path that leads to His promise. One of my personal favorite passages is found in the book of Proverbs.

Lean on, trust in, *and* be confident in the Lord with all your heart *and* mind and do not rely on your own insight *or* understanding. In all your ways know, recognize, *and* acknowledge Him, and He will direct and make straight *and* plain your paths (Prov. 3:5-6 AB).

Trust is key to having peace in our journey while we are waiting on the fulfillment of promises for us in God's Word. In order to truly trust God, we cannot rely on our own understanding or reasoning. We must rather depend on our revelation of who God is to us. We cannot truly trust someone until we know them. As our revelation of God increases, through cultivating a strong relationship with Him and reading the Word, the more trust we have. We

will discuss the importance of complete trust in week three of our study.

In this same passage, we are instructed to recognize and acknowledge God "in all our ways" and then He will direct and "make straight and plain" our paths. So, even when we miss the mark, even when we have made wrong choices and failed to submit totally to His will for our lives, when we acknowledge Him—regardless of the road we are on—He will straighten out our path and get us back on track to His promises! *He will help us lay down our reasoning and pick up fresh revelation!*

It is not too late to step into obedience with God. He is so gracious and merciful. He allows U-turns. Trust Him! Call on Him and He will direct and, yes, even redirect your path if needed.

Remind yourself of the revelation you have been given concerning our amazing God. That revelation is powerful, uplifting, and encouraging. Keep it before you and you will be strengthened to walk out His plan and believe Him for His promises as you yield your vessel in service.

As I sat in my office at home and brought to a conclusion this first week's lesson, I jotted down a list of Who God is to me as it came to my heart. There is no particular order or reason for the list as it is written below, except that it came to me this way as I wrote it. I went back and added Scripture references for you. I feel prompted to share it with you just as it came to me from my heart:

PROCLAMATION OF THE PROMISE

My God is:

- *Omnipotent (Matt. 28:18)*
- *Omnipresent (Matt. 18:20)*
- *Omniscient (John 16:30)*
- *My Healer (Isa. 53:5)*
- *My Shield (Ps. 3:3)*
- *My Rock of Ages (Ps. 28:1)*
- *My Savior (Acts 13:23)*
- *My very present help in my times of trouble (Ps. 46:1)*
- *The Great I Am (John 8:58)*
- *The Alpha and Omega - The First and The Last (Rev. 22:13)*
- *The Living Bread (John 6:32)*
- *The True Vine (John 15:5)*
- *My Wonderful, Counselor, Everlasting Father and*
- *My Prince of Peace (Isa. 9:6)*
- *My Refuge and Fortress (Ps. 91:2)*
- *My Light in Darkness (John 1:5)*
- *My Advocate (1 John 2:1)*
- *My Lord of lords and King of kings (1 Tim. 6:15)*
- *Coming back for me! (John 14:3)*
- *And through Him, no weapon formed against me shall prosper! (Isa. 54:17)*
- *And with Him I can do all things! (Phil. 4:13)*
- *And nothing, anywhere ever, can separate me from His love! (Rom. 8:38)*

- *And He will never leave me or forsake me! (Heb. 13:5)*
- *And with Him and through Him, all things are possible! (Matt. 19:26)*

Take a few moments and do the same as I did. Write down Who God is to you from your heart. Express it in your own words and in your own way:

_____

_____

_____

_____

_____

_____

_____

_____

_____

_____

_____

_____

_____

_____

_____

The list of attributes concerning the revelation truth of our God could go on and on! Each verse referenced above could be a message in itself. Each phrase describing God is reassuring and powerful.

Victory is assured and the promises of His Word that have been proclaimed will be performed in your life as you continue to walk in revelation knowledge, yielding your vessel to His purpose. As in the example

PROCLAMATION OF THE PROMISE

Mary gave, do not walk in your own strength. Do not look to yourself or your abilities to accomplish His plan. Just yield and walk in faith, fully mindful of who is in control!

As you journal and meditate this week, ask God to reveal to you again promises that are yours through the Word when you purpose to walk in obedience to Him. Ask Him for a renewed and strengthened revelation of who He is. Take the time to look up Scripture references that define the character and nature of God. And then determine to lay down your understanding as instructed in Proverbs 3:5-6 and walk in confidence that He is directing your path.

Proclaim the promise of His Word in confidence; looking with calm assurance to the One Who is able to bring it to completion. Lay down your reasoning and walk in revelation.

As Gabriel proclaimed the promise to Mary, the same truth applies to you. "With God nothing will be impossible."

As a vessel of honor in the Father's house, receive the promises proclaimed to you in the Word. Walk in obedience to God's plan for your life. Lay down reasoning and hold on to your revelation.

Week Two

POWER TRUTH

Week Two
POWER TRUTH
Profession of the Promise

As you walk with renewed determination to completely yield your life to God's plan, you must realize that there will be times you need a trusted friend to encourage you along the way.

In this week's lesson, we will consider the friendship of Elizabeth and Mary. We will discuss the importance of a mentor. There are times in your life that you will need a mentor and then there are times you will be the mentor to someone else.

It is so important that you are willing to receive this truth! It is vital when God opens your heart to new revelation for your life that you allow yourself to be mentored by a trusted, committed, faithful disciple of Christ and proven friend. It is also vitally important that you yield yourself to be that mentor to someone who needs you at a vulnerable time in his or her life. We are not alone in this journey and we need each other.

Sometimes I am the one needing a friend and other times, I am the friend someone needs!

"Again I say to you, that if two of you agree on earth about anything that they may ask, it

shall be done for them by My Father who is in heaven. For where two or three have gathered together in My name, there I am in their midst" (Matt. 18:19-20 NASB).

PROFESSION OF THE PROMISE

Week Two

PROFESSION OF THE PROMISE

Week Two
PROFESSION OF THE PROMISE
Of Mary to Elizabeth
Luke 1:39-44

God knows our needs. When He calls or directs us to walk in a path that is unfamiliar or unsettling, He often sends a strong believer who has walked in that way to mentor us. He sends someone that understands where we are to encourage and help strengthen us for the journey we have begun.

While Mary's proclamation and promise were uniquely her own and no one would have experienced anything exactly like what she had, God knew He could depend on Elizabeth to mentor and encourage Mary. He knew Elizabeth's deep revelation of God and it was apparent to all who knew her. Elizabeth had received her own personal miracle and was also fulfilling prophecy by bringing her son into the world. Because Elizabeth's son, John, would be the voice proclaiming the coming of the Messiah! How appropriate that God would orchestrate Mary and Elizabeth coming together to share their revelations. *Read again Luke 1:36-37:*

Now indeed, Elizabeth your relative has also conceived a son in her old age; and this is now the sixth month for her who was called barren. For with God nothing will be impossible (vv. 36-37).

God instructed Gabriel to share this information about Elizabeth with Mary. What better person than Elizabeth, Mary's own cousin, to encourage Mary for the journey ahead. Elizabeth was also experiencing a supernatural miracle. She had conceived a son in her old age after being barren for many years. Yes, she was going to give birth to John the Baptist! And Elizabeth's miracle would also confirm the proclamation of the promise to Mary. *Let's read Luke 1:39-44*:

> Now Mary arose in those days and went into the hill country with haste, to a city of Judah, and entered the house of Zacharias and greeted Elizabeth. And it happened, when Elizabeth heard the greeting of Mary, that the babe leaped in her womb; and Elizabeth was filled with the Holy Spirit. Then she spoke out with a loud voice and said, "Blessed *are* you among women, and blessed is the fruit of your womb! But why is this *granted* to me, that the mother of my Lord should come to me? For indeed, as soon as the voice of your greeting sounded in my ears, the babe leaped in my womb for joy (vv.39-44).

This passage tells us that immediately after the proclamation of the promise to Mary from Gabriel, that she "arose and went with haste" to Elizabeth's house in Judah. There are two things in verses 39 and 40 that we will discuss that are very important

PROFESSION OF THE PROMISE

to us as God's vessels in these last days. First, Mary immediately sought out Elizabeth! She went to Elizabeth knowing that she would find someone who would help her guard and cherish her revelation and give her the confirmation she needed. Secondly, she went with a heart that was rejoicing over the proclamation given her. Elizabeth lived in Judah, a town located in the hill country. "Judah" means praise. We should all run "with haste" to the hills of praise when we receive a proclamation of a promise from God. Praising Him in advance of receiving the promise indicates that you have picked up your revelation and are moving forward in your faith, believing in your heart.

I love Mary's story. My heart rejoices with her as I read and reflect on what it must have been like for her as the revelation of what Gabriel proclaimed settled in her heart and spirit. Mary's story and her submitted life to God is truly one of the most powerful examples of a committed vessel in the Word of God. She exemplified a vessel of honor on every level. She was clean, yielded, and accessible to God's purpose. She was able and willing to take the heat that would certainly come as a result of walking on a sometimes bumpy road that would lead to the promise. What a perfect example for us to follow!

However, I believe even Mary needed a close friend and trusted mentor. She would need someone to stand with her when the days were hard. She would need someone to pour into her heart and encourage her to hold on to her revelation when she felt pulled

toward her own reasoning and logic. She would need someone to help hold her up in prayer and in faith. She would need a faithful friend she could cry with and laugh with when others would forsake her. She would need someone who would remind her of the beautiful promise she had been given. She would need someone to remind her of the proclamation over her life.

God, in all of His infinite wisdom and in His great love for Mary, knew that she would need an encourager for the days, weeks, and months ahead leading up to the fulfillment of the promise in her life. I believe God wanted Mary to have a true friend, someone she could depend on, be real with, and trust! He wanted her to have a wise, dependable, and pure vessel to be a role model for her to safely follow and imitate. He knew Elizabeth would guard Mary's revelation and encourage her to hold on to it and not lean to her reasoning or the logic and skepticism of others. He wanted Elizabeth to pour into Mary's young and tender heart.

There are two things to consider here. There are times in your life that you will need a mentor and then there are times you will be the mentor for someone else. It is so important that you are willing to receive this truth. It is so vital when God opens your heart to new revelation that you allow yourself to be mentored by a trusted, committed, and faithful disciple of Christ and proven friend. And it is also vitally important that you yield yourself to be that mentor to someone who needs you at a vulnerable

PROFESSION OF THE PROMISE

time in their life. We are not alone in this journey and we need each other!

Sometimes I am the one needing a friend and other times, I am the friend someone needs!

There are times that you need someone to help you hold on to your revelation. You need someone of like faith that will pour into your heart and encourage you to keep the truth of what has been revealed to you alive in your spirit. You will need someone to help you refrain from trying to figure out all the details that would open you up to your own reasoning.

Remember, logic never sees or understands the unlimited power of God. Logic will often cause you to reason away the revelation.

Your mentor will need to be a true friend and one who will hold you up in prayer. This person will need to be someone who gives you a Scripture or word of encouragement when you need it most. Your mentor should be one who reminds you faithfully of what God has spoken into your life. A caring mentor will monitor their words carefully while speaking to you so that their words always reflect His! Your mentor should also be someone who loves you enough to be honest with you even if it requires a word of rebuke or correction to help get you back on the right path. Your mentor will walk in covenant with you. A real mentor is a friend you can be spiritually accountable

to in your walk with God. The value of a true mentor is priceless!

Another very important characteristic in a true mentor is that she is not jealous of God's promise and favor on your life. Elizabeth rejoiced with Mary. Elizabeth knew that Mary was highly favored of the Lord and declared like Gabriel that she was "blessed among all women" for the plans God had for her life. Instead of being envious, Elizabeth was humbled and grateful that Mary came to her for confirmation and reassurance. What a wonderful example also provided to us through Elizabeth!

Remember, pots and pans in our kitchen don't concern themselves or become jealous or envious over the use of the pot next to it. They are only concerned with their own assignment.

Think of someone who has mentored you and the value they brought to you in your walk with Christ. Perhaps it was a Sunday School teacher when you were just a child. Maybe your mentor was a relative or co-worker, someone who spoke just the right word at the right time to help you through a difficult place in your journey.

A mentor is a wonderful and helpful "ingredient" given to us by God.

Again, sometimes we are the one needing a friend and other times, we are the friend someone needs. If

PROFESSION OF THE PROMISE

you are the mentor, be sure you are a true and faithful friend and always be ready to speak encouragement and reassurance based on the Word of God. Always be trustworthy, never repeating things shared in confidence.

Read Ephesians 4:29 and consider the instruction given in this verse:

Do not let any unwholesome talk come out of your mouths, but only what is helpful for building others up according to their needs, that it may benefit those who listen (v. 29 NIV).

What do you think this verse says to you about the importance of our words?

_____

_____

_____

_____

_____

_____

_____

_____

_____

_____

A Point to Ponder: Our words can heal or hurt⊠motivate or mutilate! A kind word is soothing to the soul and dessert for the emotions. Be sweet when you speak! Your kindness will strengthen and encourage others in their journey.

In Colossians 3:16-17, we are instructed to receive "the word of Christ" and let it dwell richly in us. We are to speak wisely to others from the revelation word we have received concerning Christ. His word brings truth, understanding, and wisdom. It is from that understanding that we are to teach and admonish others.

Let the word of Christ dwell in you richly as you teach and admonish one another with all wisdom, and as you sing psalms, hymns and spiritual songs with gratitude in your hearts to God. And whatever you do, whether in word or deed, do it all in the name of the Lord Jesus, giving thanks to God the Father through him (vv. 16-17 NIV 1984).

In your own words, write a brief prayer to the Lord asking Him to help you to read and retain His Word in your heart and for Him to give you the opportunity to use His Word to mentor and help others.

_____
_____
_____
_____
_____
_____
_____
_____
_____
_____

PROFESSION OF THE PROMISE

Another powerful reminder in Colossians is found in the verse below:

> Let your conversation be always full of grace, seasoned with salt, so that you may know how to answer everyone (Col. 4:6 NIV).

It is so important that we always instruct or mentor others with words that are full of grace. We must show genuine love and concern for those we address or our words will not be received. In 1 Corinthians 13, known as the "love chapter," read how this passage begins:

> If I speak in the tongues of men and of angels, but do not have love, I am only a resounding gong or a clanging cymbal (v. 1 NIV 1984).

People know if you love them! They can tell if you are speaking in love or out of anger or to prove a point. We are not given the Word of God for the use of justifying our opinions or validating our stand on issues. The Word of God is our written revelation of Him. It is given to demonstrate and reach the lost by revealing God's love for us. We are to do the same in our speech and conduct. We are to speak the truth in love to all we meet especially those we are mentoring.

We discussed the ministry gifts Christ has given to us as listed in Ephesians 4 in last week's study. Those gifts are so important. It is also noted in that chapter

that these gifts are to be administered by speaking the truth in love if they are to be received. Let's read it in the Amplified Version:

> Rather, let our lives lovingly express truth [in all things, speaking truly, dealing truly, living truly]. Enfolded in love, let us grow up in every way and in all things into Him Who is the Head, [even] Christ (the Messiah, the Anointed One) (Eph. 4:15 AB).

As a follower of Jesus and a mentor to others, we are told to let our lives lovingly express truth. We are to be enfolded in love and grow in our relationship with Christ and lead others to do the same. Just as Elizabeth was an example to Mary, we are to be to those we meet and come in contact with on a daily basis. Who knows what may be planted in the heart of a young believer or new convert that you are influencing? You may be mentoring someone who will lead countless others to Christ! Be sure that you always mentor with genuine love so that those listening will receive your words.

The Word of God tells us in Luke 1:56 that Mary stayed with Elizabeth for about three months before she returned home. During those three months, no doubt, Mary and Elizabeth had many conversations. I can imagine that there were times when Mary was wrestling with her own emotions and fear would overcome her. She had time to think of how her family and friends in Nazareth would react to her

PROFESSION OF THE PROMISE

news. She probably put herself in their place and wondered if she would believe the story if it had been told to her by one of them. Yes, Mary would have had time to ponder and consider during those three months at Elizabeth's home all that was ahead of her in this journey she had begun. *The unknown can be so frightening to all of us.*

Imagine with me one of those nights when Mary couldn't sleep for thinking of what was ahead. She was restless and apprehensive as she thought about facing those at home. She was so young and was feeling the weight of the responsibilities she had accepted. Perhaps she secretly doubted her ability to carry out such a great task.

She found herself getting up in the night and moving quietly to a chair at a small table in the corner of the room. The only light in the room was that of a lantern flickering on the wall. She sat at the table, elbows propped on it, with her face in her hands.

Elizabeth was also unable to sleep, awakened by her own discomfort, for her time of delivery was approaching. She saw Mary sitting quietly, and knowing she was troubled, went to her.

In my imagination, I see Elizabeth pull up a chair and move close to Mary. She put her hand lovingly on her shoulder and softly said, "Mary, fear not. The Holy Spirit is with you. Our Father would never require of you anything without giving you the strength you would need to walk it out. He will perform this great promise He has made to you. You

have willingly submitted your vessel of obedience to Him. The rest He will do. You do not have to concern yourself with the details. Our Great Heavenly Father has already taken care of them. Trust Him, Mary, He will be with you throughout this journey. He will instruct and guide you every step of the way."

Perhaps Mary's reply would be, "But Elizabeth, what if they do not believe what was told to me by the angel of the Lord? What if they doubt me? And Elizabeth, I am going home to Nazareth. The Messiah is to be born in Bethlehem.

There is just so much I do not understand and so much as yet to be explained to me. There are more questions than answers for what lies ahead for me."

I believe Elizabeth would have responded like this, "Sweet Mary, do not allow yourself to be fearful. Remember the angel declared to you that you were highly favored and blessed. Remember he told you not to fear. Do not be troubled in your heart for what others may think, for you know the truth. You have received divine revelation from God Himself! Hold tightly to your revelation. Do not pick up your reasoning and become afraid. Mary, put your hand here, feel my baby move, he will soon be here. He was your sign, your confirmation that you had heard truth from Gabriel. You are blessed with a wonderful promise! Do not let fear rob you of the joy that comes with knowing God has an eternal and great plan for you. Let your heart rejoice again as it did the day you shared your promise with me. All is well,

Mary. The Father is with you! Remember the angel's words⊠'with God all things are possible!'"

In my heart, I believe they embraced and Mary found strength and comfort from the love and words of her friend and mentor. I believe Mary found solace and peace from her encouragement and she pondered the wisdom of Elizabeth's words many times in the days and months ahead.

I truly believe that Elizabeth's words to Mary were always seasoned with grace and love. She was willing and ready to speak comfort and strength into the heart of Mary. She was a true mentor.

Read the verses below carefully and let them settle deeply in your heart.

Since by your obedience to the Truth *through the [Holy] Spirit* you have purified your hearts for the sincere affection of the brethren, [see that you] love one another fervently from a *pure* heart (1 Peter 1:22 AB).

Little children, let us not love [merely] in theory *or* in speech but in deed and in truth (in practice and in sincerity) (1 John 3:18 AB).

Now, take a moment and write what you feel these verses are speaking to you:

_____

_____

_____

_____

_____

_____

_____

_____

_____

Let's take another look at more verses concerning love in 1 Corinthians 13:

> Love endures long *and* is patient and kind; love never is envious *nor* boils over with jealousy, is not boastful *or* vainglorious, does not display itself haughtily. It is not conceited (arrogant and inflated with pride); it is not rude (unmannerly) and does not act unbecomingly. Love (God's love in us) does not insist on its own rights *or* its own way, *for* it is not self-seeking; it is not touchy *or* fretful *or* resentful; it takes no account of the evil done to it [it pays no attention to a suffered wrong]. It does not rejoice at injustice *and* unrighteousness, but rejoices when right and truth prevail. Love bears up under anything *and* everything that comes, is ever ready to believe the best of every person, its hopes are fadeless under all circumstances, and it endures everything [without weakening] (vv. 4-7 AB).

When mentoring someone, these verses can be so beneficial and become a true set of guidelines to measure the strength of our love. Remember, we must continually demonstrate love or our words will not be received.

PROFESSION OF THE PROMISE

When I read this passage I understand that love is not always easy to give. These verses explain love in a clear and simple way. It begins by saying what love *is not* so that we will know what true love really *is*. It reminds us that love is not conceited or prideful. It is not rude and does not act badly. It is not demanding or insistent on getting its way. Love does not search out for things that satisfy its own wants without regarding others. Love does not tend to act moody or fretful or display a bad attitude or show resentment and real love does not keep an account, nor does it ever keep a list of things done wrong to it. It does not rejoice over wrong, ever. It does not take joy in things that are unrighteous. Those are things love will not do.

Oh but look at what love does! It rejoices when right and truth win out. Love bears anything it is required to carry. Regardless of what comes its way, it endures just the same and love is so amazing because it is always eager and ready to believe the absolute best of everyone. Real love always, always has hope regardless of the circumstances surrounding it. It is strong enough to endure the test and stress of time and trials that come and it still remains eternally strong.

A true mentor is one who will love you through the difficult places, season her words with grace and speak the truth to you when you need to hear it the most. Someone who loves you with the kind and depth of love we have seen described in these passages is someone who is to be cherished and

someone you can trust. It is that kind of person Mary found in Elizabeth. Mary was able to safely profess her promise to Elizabeth. She knew when she shared this revelation with Elizabeth, that she would guard and protect what she had revealed.

A true mentor is someone who feels honored to pour into you. Elizabeth rejoiced that Mary came to her. She was thrilled with the word Mary brought and was grateful to have the privilege of hearing Mary's profession of the promise given her.

Guard your promise carefully. Profess the promise. Profess, declare, and speak the promise based on revelation from the Word of God. When you feel your faith weakening, when you feel alone and begin to lean to your understanding, when you find yourself laying down revelation and picking up reasoning, remember you are not alone in this journey! Reach out to God and to your trusted mentor and friend. Agree together in prayer and hold on to divine revelation. Your profession will be powerful and positive and your faith will be strengthened.

Your profession of the promise must be positive! Be careful that you do not mix reasoning and doubt in with your revelation. If you do, you will begin to lean to your understanding instead of the truth you have been given concerning your promise. Your words must reflect your faith in God and your confidence that He is able to complete what He has promised.

One of my favorite verses is *Psalm 19:14*:
Let the words of my mouth and the meditation of my heart be acceptable in Your sight, O Lord, my strength and my Redeemer.

What we think and what we say are so important as we walk in this journey for the Lord. When we meditate on the things that have been revealed to us about the character and nature of God and we grow in our relationship with Him, our words will reflect that revelation. We will profess the promise the way it was given in our heart.

> *Mary professed the promise to Elizabeth just as Gabriel spoke it to her!*

Read this familiar passage of Scripture found in Matthew 18:19-20 and think about the value of a true friend and mentor who will take the time to intercede with you in agreement.

> Again I say to you, that if two of you agree on earth about anything that they may ask, it shall be done for them by My Father who is in heaven. For where two or three have gathered together in My name, there I am in their midst (NASB).

After reading and meditating on this verse, write your own thoughts concerning the value of having a mentor in your life and making yourself available as a mentor to someone:

_____

_____

_____

_____

_____

_____

_____

_____

_____

_____

We are vessels in God's house! We have been made clean through our relationship with Christ. We are yielding ourselves to His service. We are accessible to His plan and available to Him. One way that we can be successful in our journey and in obedience is by allowing ourselves to be mentored and encouraged by a true friend and fellow disciple of Christ.

As you journal this week, remember it is vitally important as you yield your life to God's plan, that you hold tightly to your revelation of God. It is important that you profess in faith the promises you are holding in your heart. Your mentor and friend will help you to see God clearly and encourage you to hold on in faith to the promise that will be manifested through your life of obedience to God.

Ask God to help you know when you need a mentor and lead you to that one He has chosen for you. Ask Him to help you receive from them as they walk with you.

Then also ask Him to help you know when you are chosen to be the mentor and allow Him to prepare your heart to pour into that one who needs you in their journey.

PROFESSION OF THE PROMISE

When you receive a promise, guard it in
your heart carefully.

Profess it to a trusted believer who will encourage
you and mentor you through the journey you have
begun, and if someone shares their personal promise
from God with you, you prove to be that trustworthy
friend and mentor!

Remember, the value of a true mentor cannot
be measured!

Week Three

POWER TRUTH

Week Three
POWER TRUTH
Prophecy of the Promise

We will learn the importance of three ingredients needed in our vessel as we walk in obedience to God.

Trust—Hope—Patience

These are three key and necessary ingredients the Father will place in our vessels as we walk in obedience to His plan. These valuable ingredients will help us endure on our journey to the fulfillment of the promise and God's purpose for us.

> Lean on, trust in, *and* be confident in the Lord with all your heart *and* mind and do not rely on your own insight *or* understanding. In all your ways know, recognize, *and* acknowledge Him, and He will direct *and* make straight and plain your paths (Prov. 3:5-6 AB).

Week Three

PROPHECY OF THE PROMISE

Week Three
PROPHECY OF THE PROMISE
From Elizabeth to Mary
Luke 1:45

Blessed *is* she who believed, for there will be a
fulfillment of those things which were told her
from the Lord (Luke 1:45).

What an exciting move of the Spirit of God that
happened in this verse of Scripture! Prophecy had
been dormant and a new era was beginning with the
renewal of this gift. The revelation of the promise of
the coming birth of the Messiah through Mary caused
a response in Elizabeth and she gave a prophetic
word that confirmed what had been told to Mary by
Gabriel.

Hearing confirmation of promises through
prophecy will help you hold on to the revelation
you have been given. Prophecy will often confirm
what you have already heard and received in your
heart from the Word. Once we hear and *receive a
prophecy*, it reminds us that we are to walk in faith
concerning what we have heard, and in obedience to
God, while fully anticipating a performance of those
promises in our life.

Elizabeth began the prophecy by commending
Mary for her faith. She pronounced a blessing on
Mary because of that faith. She said, "Blessed is
she who believed..." Through those few words,

Elizabeth pointed out that Mary had genuine faith in the face of an amazing proclamation that would require an absolute miracle. Faith, especially for those things that truly seem impossible, is always to be commended and God always rewards it.

Imagine the joy in Mary's heart as she heard the confirmation of the proclamation that had been given to her by God through Gabriel. Elizabeth prophesied through the revelation of the Holy Spirit to Mary. Mary's heart rejoiced and so did Elizabeth's.

The gift of prophecy brings edification and comfort to those hearing and receiving the prophetic declaration from the Spirit of God.

Read 1 Corinthians 14:3. The gift of prophecy comforts and strengthens. It brings encouragement and hope and serves as a reminder that God is continually aware of us and is constantly mindful of the things that concern us. It is for the purpose of bringing spiritual progress in the life of the hearer.

> But he who prophesies speaks edification and exhortation and comfort to men (v. 3).

Prophecy is a divinely inspired and anointed word from God.

Prophecy is also for the purpose of giving clear vision and revelation, and for increasing and awakening expectations concerning the promises in the Word. When revelation is given and expectations are renewed through the gift of

PROPHECY OF THE PROMISE

prophecy, complacency is replaced by revived hope and obedience to God.

A word of prophecy is also a sign to the believer that God is present and mindful of them. This brings comfort to the believer and if a sinner is present, it simultaneously brings conviction often bringing them to repentance.

A Point to Ponder: In these last days, there are many voices who proclaim they are speaking on behalf of God and under the direction of the Spirit of God. Always remember the description and purpose of a true word of prophecy as presented in 1 Corinthians 14:3. And be aware that a true prophetic word *never* contradicts the written Word of God!

The various gifts of the Spirit are identified in *1 Corinthians 12:4-11*. Pay special attention to verse 7. In this verse, we are reminded that the gifts, though diverse, are all for the benefit of the body of Christ.

There are different kinds of gifts, but the same Spirit distributes them. There are different kinds of service, but the same Lord. There are different kinds of working, but in all of them and in everyone it is the same God at work. Now to each one the manifestation of the Spirit is given for the common good. To one there is given through the Spirit a message of wisdom, to another a message of knowledge by means

of the same Spirit, to another faith by the same Spirit, to another gifts of healing by that one Spirit, to another miraculous powers, to another prophecy, to another distinguishing between spirits, to another speaking in different kinds of tongues, and to still another the interpretation of tongues. All these are the work of one and the same Spirit, and he distributes them to each one, just as he determines (vv. 4-11 NIV).

The gifts of the Spirit are so important in building the Kingdom of God. We are to pursue love and desire spiritual gifts (1 Corinthians 14:1). Our motives for having these gifts are always for the benefit of the body of Christ and furthering the Gospel of Christ.

Also be mindful that the gift of prophecy is never for the purpose of bringing glory to the one giving the prophetic word. Remember, the pots and pans never take credit for what is produced in them. All glory goes to God!

Again, once we hear and *receive a prophecy*, it reminds us that we are to walk in faith concerning what we have heard and in obedience to God while fully anticipating a performance of those promises in our life. When things get difficult and the wait seems long, the prophecy serves as a confirmation and a reference point that brings reassurance that we are on the right path.

PROPHECY OF THE PROMISE

We discussed in the first week of our study how it might have been if Mary had stepped into reasoning and laid down her revelation concerning what had been proclaimed over her life. As a vessel yielded to God's plan, we must not fall into the trap of feeling that we have to "make it happen" for God.

Patience in the process from the time of the proclamation and prophecy of the promise to the performance of it is necessary!

As a vessel used for God's purpose, I must yield my life and walk in obedience. In patience I must wait for a performance of the promise, assured that it will be a reality.

Trust is an absolute necessity in our walk of obedience. There are many things we face that we will not understand. There are problems we will have to deal with and pain we experience in our journey. If we walk without absolute trust in God, we will begin to lose our patience, become weary, and begin to doubt our choice to submit to His plan. *However, if we walk in trust and revelation of Him, we know we will endure and the results of obedience will be rewarded.*

Let's look again at Proverbs 3:5-6 and the importance of trust:

Lean on, trust in, *and* be confident in the Lord with all your heart *and* mind and do not rely on your own insight *or* understanding. In all your

ways know, recognize, *and* acknowledge Him, and He will direct and make straight *and* plain your paths (AB).

As we discussed previously, *trust is essential in order to have peace in our journey* while we are waiting on the fulfillment of the promises in God's Word for us. We cannot rely on our own understanding! We must depend on and refer to our revelation of who God is to us. We must remember the Word of God concerning a life of obedience.

Take a moment and, from your heart, write a simple prayer asking God to help you walk in complete confidence in His ability to bring to pass what He has promised. Ask Him to strengthen your trust in Him as you walk in obedience to His plan for your life:

_____

_____

_____

_____

_____

_____

_____

_____

_____

_____

_____

_____

_____

_____

PROPHECY OF THE PROMISE

Like Mary did, you are to hold tightly to that word of prophecy that may have been given concerning your life, but, you may feel that you haven't been given a "spoken word" confirming your call or a promise from God. The written Word of God will direct and confirm in your heart God's plan for you! The Word is available to us and given for us so that we may know Him and serve Him. Study the Word and know God through it. The more you know Him, the more you trust Him. The more you know His Word, the more you are assured of His will for your life.

Also, trust in God will enable you to handle the ingredients you may have placed in your vessel. In the introduction we mentioned various types of ingredients that are used to prepare a recipe. Some are bitter, some sweet, and some bland—but all may be necessary to accomplish the goal of the chef. There are *ingredients* that we would rather not have to deal with as we yield our vessel to God, but we must trust God that He will work all things to our good and the end results will be worth it.

In our "living pots and pans," we imagined that they would never want a tasteless or bitter or sour or bland ingredient placed in them, and we are the same! We would rather everything be sweet and bring joy in our journey, but in life we face all sorts of situations—some are difficult, some are painful and we would certainly rather not be faced with them. The enemy would love to distract us and get us off course so that we will not walk according to

God's purpose. Both trust and patience will help us deal with the ingredients that may be challenging us in our walk with God.

A Point to Ponder: In these last days, there are many voices that proclaim they are speaking on behalf of God and under the direction of the Spirit of God. Always remember the description and purpose of a true word of prophecy as presented in 1 Corinthians 14:3. Be aware that a true prophetic word *never* contradicts the written Word of God!

As we have already discussed, Proverbs 3:5-6 reminds us that trusting in God, laying down our reasoning, and looking to Him assures us that He will direct our path. *We can take comfort knowing that any path God leads us on will end in a good place!*

Read Isaiah 26:3-4. This beautiful and comforting passage reminds us of just some of the rewards that come as a benefit of trusting God.

You will guard him *and* keep him in perfect *and* constant peace whose mind [both its inclination and its character] is stayed on You, because he commits himself to You, leans on You, *and* hopes confidently in You. So trust in the Lord (commit yourself to Him, lean on Him, hope confidently in Him) forever; for the Lord God is an everlasting Rock [the Rock of Ages] (AB).

PROPHECY OF THE PROMISE

We are promised if we keep our minds in tune with and on God, keeping revelation knowledge of Him in the forefront of our thoughts, that He will guard and keep our minds in a constant state of peace. We are instructed to trust the Lord and trust comes easily when our mind is continually on God. We are to commit to Him our ways, lean on Him for assurance and power to carry out our commitment to Him, and hope in Him for all things. How can we do that? Because He is the unchanging, immoveable, everlasting God, and our eternal Rock of Ages. He has promised that He will never leave us or forsake us!

When we are constantly walking in the awareness of God's strength, character, ability and love for us, we have perfect and constant peace and trust in Him comes easily!

Read Jeremiah 17:7-8. These verses also assure us that our trust in God brings great benefits!

[Most] blessed is the man who believes in, trusts in, *and* relies on the Lord, and whose hope *and* confidence the Lord is. For he shall be like a tree planted by the waters that spreads out its roots by the river; and it shall not see *and* fear when heat comes; but its leaf shall be green. It shall not be anxious and full of care in the year of drought, nor shall it cease yielding fruit (AB).

This passage reminds us that we are blessed when we trust God and our hope and our confidence are always in Him. We are assured that we will be stable and strong when troubles come because our roots and foundation are in God. We will not fear when the heat of trials surrounds us. We will not be filled with dread or worry when problems arise and none of these things will prevent us from bearing fruit in our journey with God.

My confidence and trust must be in God and not in my own strength!

In our walk of obedience, it is imperative that we do not rely on our own talents, strength or abilities. Our confidence must be in Him and His power working through us. If we are blessed with talents, we must remember He has allowed us to have them and they are His gift to use through our obedience to bless the body of Christ. If we become dependent on our strengths, talents and abilities and enjoy some measure of success in ministry, we open ourselves up to pride and become vulnerable to the enemy. Our confidence and hope must be in God alone and all glory must go to Him. This prevents pride from being our downfall.

My confidence and trust in God will enable me to overcome my fear of failure!

PROPHECY OF THE PROMISE

Also, we must never be afraid of our own weaknesses and use our inabilities and limitations to keep us from walking in our purpose. When we focus on our weaknesses, we tend to become fearful because of our lack of talents or strengths in certain areas. We become insecure and also give access to our mind into the divisive and destructive plans of the enemy. Intimidation from the enemy will prevent us from walking in our purpose.

The enemy doesn't care how he defeats you. He just wants to defeat you. He will cause you to crumble because of pride or crush you because of insecurities. He wants to rob you of the joy of obedience and the beautiful promises that result from your God-given purpose being fulfilled.

But the devil cannot destroy you when your confidence is in God and in Him alone!

When you are walking in the revelation of the power and abilities of God and trusting that He will be with you, the devil cannot stop you. Just like Mary did, you will walk in obedience and God will birth through you His plan for your life and many will be blessed.

When our confidence is in God, we are planted firmly on a solid foundation; when troubles come and the winds blow, we will remain. Those who trust God will not worry or be alarmed when battles are raging and nothing will prevent them from producing fruit.

The enemy wants to rob you of your hope in the future. He wants to make you feel as if God's promises will never be realized in your life. If he is able to rob you of your hope for the future, he makes you feel powerless in your present. True trust births hope and hope will not let you give up in your obedience to God. So true hope in His promise births patience. We will wait for the fulfillment of those promises when we are assured that fulfillment is coming!

Trust in God births hope and hope births patience!

Let's read Romans 8:25-28. In this familiar and loved chapter, Paul reminds and assures us that all things work together for good for and to those who love God and are called according to His design and purpose. All the ingredients will work for our good. God has an amazing ability to take what the enemy means for our harm and turn it around for our benefit!

Notice verse 25 and the instruction given. We are to hope for what is unseen and wait for it with patience. The next verses tell us how we can do what sounds and sometimes feels impossible. The Holy Spirit comes to our aid! He bears us up when we are weak. He prays on our behalf when we don't know how to pray or what to even ask for. He intercedes and pleads on behalf of us in accordance to God's will for our life. Because of this, we have our beloved promise found in verse 28!

PROPHECY OF THE PROMISE

But if we hope for what is still unseen by us, we wait for it with patience *and* composure. So too the [Holy] Spirit comes to our aid *and* bears us up in our weakness; for we do not know what prayer to offer *nor* how to offer it worthily as we ought, but the Spirit Himself goes to meet our supplication *and* pleads in our behalf with unspeakable yearnings *and* groanings too deep for utterance. And He Who searches the hearts of men knows what is in the mind of the [Holy] Spirit [what His intent is], because the Spirit intercedes *and* pleads [before God] in behalf of the saints according to *and* in harmony with God's will. We are assured *and* know that [God being a partner in their labor] all things work together *and* are [fitting into a plan] for good to *and* for those who love God and are called according to [His] design *and* purpose (Rom. 8:25-28 AB).

Read and meditate on Romans 8:25 and write down in your own words why you feel hope will cause you to have "patience and composure" while you are waiting on the promises:

_____

_____

_____

_____

_____

_____

_____

Hope comes as a result of revelation knowledge about God! We can truly have hope when we walk in the revelation of truth. Our God cannot lie! Our God cannot fail! If God's Word declares it as truth—it is truth! Hope in Him and you will never be disappointed. The hope that resides in you will cause you to endure with patience for the promise because nothing and no one will be able to take your hope from you when you base it on His eternal unchanging Word.

Read Psalm 42:5. The psalmist addresses himself in this verse. He asks himself why he is cast down and his soul in despair. He instructs himself to hope in God. He is to wait in full expectation and faith. He is to wait with praise in his heart. Praise is given because hope already believes for the promise though yet unattained in the natural. How? Because God is my Help and He cannot and will not fail!

> Why are you cast down, O my inner self? And why should you moan over me and be disquieted within me? Hope in God and wait expectantly for Him, for I shall yet praise Him, my Help and my God. (Ps. 42:5 AB).

Hope is powerful and hope gives birth to patience! Patience is a word we tend to want to avoid, but as vessels in God's house, for His use, we must have patience to endure. *Just as we have discussed the importance and the need for trust and hope, we will see the value and rewards of patience!*

PROPHECY OF THE PROMISE

Read Luke 8:11-15. In these verses, Jesus is giving His explanation of the Parable of the Sower.

> Now the parable is this: The seed is the word of God. Those by the wayside are the ones who hear; then the devil comes and takes away the word out of their hearts, lest they should believe and be saved. But the ones on the rock *are those* who, when they hear, receive the word with joy; and these have no root, who believe for a while and in time of temptation fall away. Now the ones *that* fell among thorns are those who, when they have heard, go out and are choked with cares, riches, and pleasures of life, and bring no fruit to maturity. But the ones *that* fell on the good ground are those who, having heard the word with a noble and good heart, keep *it* and bear fruit with patience (vv.11-15).

The seed represents the Word of God. As we read, we see how the enemy desires to steal away the seed before it takes root. He is successful in doing so, except in the seeds that fell on "good ground" as described in verse 15. Those who heard the Word and hold tightly to it bear fruit from that seed when they endure with patience.

We cannot abort the promise by giving up too soon! Hope will cause us to endure with patience and the results bring forth the promise.

Read Hebrews 10:35-36. This passage tells us not to throw away our confidence in God, because it

brings with it wonderful and glorious compensations. We have to hold on with steadfast patience and endurance, determined to accomplish the will of God and our purpose. When we do, we will carry away the fullness of what had been promised as a result of obedience.

> Do not, therefore, fling away your fearless confidence, for it carries a great *and* glorious compensation of reward. For you have need of steadfast patience *and* endurance, so that you may perform *and* fully accomplish the will of God, and thus receive *and* carry away [and enjoy to the full] what is promised (Heb. 10:35-36 AB).

You may say, "I would never throw away my fearless confidence in God!" However, when we lose heart because of becoming restless while waiting, when we get tired and give up before obtaining what was promised, we are actually saying with our actions that we have lost confidence in God.

In Hebrews 10:36, we are told we have need of steadfast patience and endurance. The word "steadfast" means to be fixed, firmly established, resolute, and unwavering! Write your own thoughts about the rewards we are assured according to this verse as a result of having that kind of patience:

_____

_____

_____

PROPHECY OF THE PROMISE

_____

_____

_____

_____

_____

Read James 1:3-4. Patience may be developed through trials and not losing faith in times of struggle and longsuffering, but the rewards are worth it. Look at verse 4. When patience has completed its work in us, we are a people complete and lacking in nothing. Patience is a wonderful characteristic that reaps great benefits.

> Be assured *and* understand that the trial *and* proving of your faith bring out endurance *and* steadfastness *and* patience. But let endurance *and* steadfastness *and* patience have full play *and* do a thorough work, so that you may be [people] perfectly and fully developed [with no defects], lacking in nothing (James 1:3-4 AB).

Patience is a misunderstood ingredient! It is not an optional part of the recipe. For successful results in the yielded vessel, patience is required. However, we often shy away from it when we feel God wants to increase our patience, because patience is often cultivated and strengthened through trials and struggles. Very few people are just naturally patient! We cannot deny the importance of having patience in our nature and conduct once we fully understand its tremendous rewards.

As I was studying and praying about this week's lesson, I asked God to help me see and understand characteristics of patience. This is what I wrote in my journal after praying for understanding. I felt I should share as a part of this lesson.

Patience in spiritual warfare is not a complacent mindset declaring defeat. It is not a feeling of doom and dread because of the anticipation of failure. It is not a constant fight with your emotions or a state of frustration. It is not "sitting still in the corner" because you are overwhelmed, weary, burdened or too tired to fight.

No, patience is a calm and confident mindset, knowing God is working on your behalf, completely expecting and anticipating victory! When genuine patience becomes part of our character, it is truly a place of refuge and calm, and provides a place of rest! Patience is a place where the battle worn soldier of faith can rest in revelation knowledge and hear the Father whisper, "Relax, my beloved daughter, for I will go and bring forth what I have promised. Rest assured, for I am faithful to My Word. Be still and know that I am God!"

Yes, patience is a gift from God! Don't be afraid when you feel Him leading you to acquire more of it. The results are worth it!

As we continue to study Mary's journey, we will see how she demonstrated her trust in God and her hope in Him. We will see that she endured

with patience to the time of the performance of the promise proclaimed to her. We must do the same. As vessels of God—clean, accessible, and trusting God with the ingredients—we must cultivate trust, hope, and patience through increased revelation of God. We will discuss ingredients that we must deal with in greater detail in week five's study.

Trust—Hope—Patience

These are three key and necessary ingredients the Father will place in our vessels as we walk in obedience to His plan. These valuable ingredients will help us endure and make it to the fulfillment of the promise and accomplishing our purpose.

When Mary heard the prophecy confirming what God had revealed to her through Elizabeth, she was encouraged and strengthened. You also can receive that assurance through the Word of God and go forward with trust in Him, fully confident that He is faithful to complete what He has promised. Your trust in Him will bring forth hope and as your hope is strengthened you will endure with patience knowing the promise is coming. For He is faithful that promised!

So let us seize *and* hold fast *and* retain without wavering the hope we cherish *and* confess *and* our acknowledgement of it, for He Who promised is reliable (sure) *and* faithful to His word (Heb. 10:23 AB).

As you spend time journaling this week, write down your thoughts concerning the importance of having the ingredients of trust, hope, and patience in your vessel as you walk in obedience to God. Ask the Lord to strengthen you in the areas where you may be weak concerning trust, hope, and patience.

Go back over parts of this week's study and the Scriptures referenced. Commit to memory those verses that minister to you and speak to your heart.

When you receive confirmation of God's plan for your life from the preached or printed Word of God or through the gift of prophecy, hold tightly to that assurance. Walk, trusting in God, with your hope confident in Him. Let patience be birthed in your heart through that hope, knowing it will be completed. For He is faithful that promised!

PROPHECY OF THE PROMISE

Week Four

POWER TRUTH

Week Four
POWER TRUTH
Praise for the Promise

In this week's lesson, we will be reminded of the importance of praise as a daily part of our life in our walk of obedience.

Praise must be a priority in the life of a yielded vessel! Praise causes us to focus on Him. As He is magnified in our hearts through worship, so are His strengths and abilities. Words of praise, as they are declaring the greatness of God and His faithfulness, actually increase the faith of the one speaking them.

> *Make praise a priority in your daily walk with God. Praise for God is another "ingredient" we need in our vessel!*

Sing praises to God, sing praises! Sing praises to our King, sing praises! For God is the King of all the earth; Sing praises with understanding (Ps. 47:6-7).

Week Four

PRAISE FOR THE PROMISE

PRAISE FOR THE PROMISE
From Mary to God
Luke 1:46-55

In this week's lesson, we will discuss the importance of praise. We will see the blessings that come when heartfelt praise is given and exemplified in the life of a believer and in our walk of obedience to Him.

As we continue with Mary's story according to the gospel of Luke, we will see how genuine, heartfelt praise is given from Mary to God. From your Bible, read over the "song of Mary" recorded in Luke 1:46-55.

This beautiful passage allows us a glimpse into the heart of Mary as she expresses her gratitude to God. Mary's praise was powerful and sincere. Her joy was full. God and He alone was the object of her worship and adoration.

Let's look closely at Luke 1:46-47:

And Mary said: "My soul magnifies the Lord,
And my spirit has rejoiced in God my Savior."

Mary began her song of praise by saying, "My soul magnifies the Lord, and my spirit has rejoiced in God my Savior!" She was celebrating the great revelation from God and was also rejoicing in the wonderful confirmation by the Spirit of God through Elizabeth. With her heart full of praise, Mary's focus

was now on the need of expressing her gratitude to the One who had made this all possible. She could go no further until she stopped and gave thanks to Him. Nothing else mattered at the moment. Mary's spirit was rejoicing and *she made praise a priority!*

Praise must be a priority in the life of a yielded vessel! Praise causes us to focus on Him. As He is magnified in our hearts through worship, so are His strengths and abilities. Words of praise, as they are declaring the greatness of God and His faithfulness, actually increase the faith of the one speaking them.

> *Make praise a priority in your daily walk*
> *with God! Praise for God is another*
> *ingredient we need in our vessel.*

The word "magnifies" in verse 46 means "declares the greatness of." In magnifying God, Mary demonstrated her great respect and high esteem for Him. In Mary's song of praise, she made God the focal point of her worship and in doing so, she would have also caused Elizabeth to praise God as she witnessed and heard Mary's words.

A Point to Ponder: In our church services, praise through music is a very real and vital part of our worship. Singers and musicians desire to give their very best to Him. Practice and preparation are essential in order to do this. But even when we are blessed with great singers and musicians leading us into worship, all praise and honor are

PRAISE FOR THE PROMISE

due Him. True worship leaders always desire to cause the focus to be on Christ and all the glory directed to Him. A true anointed worship leader rejoices when your focus is on God as a result of their efforts but if you have been blessed to enter into worship as the result of the leadership of an anointed, sincere worship leader, you know they are deserving of your appreciation for yielding to the call of God. Someone who walks in the ministry of a worship leader, as a yielded vessel to Him, is worthy of appreciation for their service to God and the church. Often, because of their vital role, they experience spiritual warfare. Expressing your appreciation to them for their efforts can go a long way in keeping them encouraged as they minister to the body of Christ!

In verse 47, Mary says, "my spirit has rejoiced in God my Savior!" Mary had yielded her life and her vessel completely to God for His plan and purpose, but she also knew that *God would reward her with blessings untold for her obedience!* She acknowledged that by saying in the following verse, "all generations will call me blessed." This made her heart cry out in thanksgiving. She was humbled and appreciative of the opportunity to serve God and grateful that she would be blessed for it.

We are to be encouraged with that same mindset. *God always blesses obedience!* Not just in the life to come, but in our daily walk here. We discussed

just a few of the promises of walking in obedience, recorded in Deuteronomy 28:2-14, in lesson one. The Word of God is filled with promises and blessings for those who are faithful!

A passage similar to Luke 1:47 is found in *Habakkuk 3:18*:

> Yet I will rejoice in the Lord, I will joy in the God of my salvation.

The word "joy" in this verse is powerful in its meaning! Its definition includes "rejoice, be glad, to be joyful" and also suggests "dancing for joy" because of revelation knowledge of God. This kind of praise is never intended for only those times in your life when all is well. *No, praise is not given only on good days!* Expressions of gratitude are not reserved for just when all is well. Praise and thanksgiving are not based on what you have been given alone, but rather on who God is and your realization that He is faithful and good.

Let's read more from this passage in Habakkuk. Now we will include Habakkuk 3:17 to illustrate this point:

> Though the fig tree does not blossom and there is no fruit on the vines, [though] the product of the olive fails and the fields yield no food, though the flock is cut off from the fold and there are no cattle in the stalls, Yet I will rejoice

PRAISE FOR THE PROMISE

in the Lord; I will exult in the [victorious] God of my salvation (vv. 17-18 AB).

This passage (Habakkuk 3:17-19) is sometimes referred to as a hymn of faith. It declares that even when there are very real problems, God is worthy of our praise. Even when there are no blossoms on the fig trees or fruit on the vines, when the olive trees are not producing and the fields are not yielding a harvest, and the stalls are empty of livestock—God is still worthy of praise.

In other words, though nothing seems to be going right and all you have labored for seems to be fruitless and you feel you have failed in all areas, *God is still God* and He is mindful of you!

The enemy would love to make you feel that you have *missed the mark* and that you are not in God's will based on all that seems to be wrong at the moment, but you must not focus on the circumstances at hand. *Focus on who God is!* Lay down reasoning and walk in revelation. That beautiful revelation is given in verse 19:

The Lord God is my Strength, my personal bravery, *and* my invincible army; He makes my feet like hinds' feet and will make me to walk [not to stand still in terror, but to walk] *and* make [spiritual] progress upon my high places [of trouble, suffering, or responsibility] (AB).

I love Habakkuk 3:19! It reminds me of how amazing and personal our God is, and that brings comfort and peace regardless of what may be happening at the moment. This verse alone gives us a glimpse of our God, His care for us and His unlimited power and strength to make the impossible a reality.

Look closely at what it says to the believer. I have written it down in my own words in my journal and made it personal. I want to share it with you. Read the following aloud:

The Lord is MY strength! The Lord is MY personal bravery! He is MY invincible army! He makes me walk—not stand terrified, unsure of what to do next—but walk confidently knowing He has gone before me and taken care of the situation. He enables me to make progress even when I am in troubled and pressing times. He ensures that I will make progress even when I am suffering and He will enable me to make needed progress in my areas of responsibility.

Take a moment and write down what Habakkuk 3:17-19 says to your heart about praise:

_____

_____

_____

_____

_____

_____

_____

Have you ever felt overwhelmed with your responsibilities? In this busy world we live in, we

Praise for the Promise

often have many roles to fill. We can feel pressed and uncertain *but God is able and ready to help us through those things that are required of us.*

You really want to fully commit to a life of complete obedience to God. You want to be that vessel that is clean, accessible, trusting God with the ingredients and able to endure the heat when it is required of you. Perhaps you are a wife and mother of young children and also working a job outside of home. Maybe you are a single mom and feel the demands of parenting alone. Maybe you are a pastor's wife and you have the weight of the responsibilities that come with full-time ministry. Perhaps you are a caregiver to an elderly parent or a spouse in poor health and you feel inadequate at times under the circumstances you are in. The descriptions of responsibilities we have may all differ, but *we all feel the same pressure from our to-do lists at times.* You feel if you add one more thing to your list it will be more than you can handle.

God desires for us to have a renewed revelation of just how much He cares about every detail of our lives and the responsibilities required of us. I have said so many times, "If He loves me enough to number the hairs on my head (see Matthew 10:30), how much more does He care about the things that can overwhelm me?"

Mary could have focused on the days of uncertainty that were ahead. She could have lost her thoughts in reasoning and her focus could have shifted from God to "what others may be going to say or think" or "what will Joseph say?" or "what will I do if

my family rejects me?" According to the law, she could have been stoned to death for being pregnant outside of marriage. She could have felt a sense of dread because of the unknown. She could have lost herself in her own thoughts of inadequacy at the thought of being a mother, and I cannot imagine the overwhelming thought of having the responsibility of nurturing and caring for the Son of God!

Mary had to lay this reasoning down and focus on God. *So do we!*

Yes, Mary could have lost her praise if she had lost her focus, and so can we! Walking in revelation awareness of Him is essential to keeping praise alive and the benefits of praise are endless.

The devil hates our praise because it is so effective against his strategy to distract and cause fear in our heart. When we praise God and we hear our own declarations concerning Him, our faith is strengthened and our fear begins to fade.

When we praise Him, He is present and personal. He is with us in our places of battle ready to be that "invincible army" on our behalf and He is with us in our places of victory, sharing in our joy.

King David of the Old Testament was a powerful man of God. He knew what it was to walk in obedience and he knew what it was to willfully disobey and fail God. David knew what it was like to succeed, and he also experienced great sorrow and grief. However, one thing David did consistently was praise, and he learned that praise often helped him regain his proper focus.

PRAISE FOR THE PROMISE

David was a gifted psalmist and he gave us so many of the wonderful songs of praise recorded in the book of Psalms. The book of Psalms begins with a description of the way of the righteous in Psalm 1. It defines those with a firm foundation and declares that they will be like a tree planted by the water and will bring forth fruit in season. Also, Psalm 150, the last recorded psalm, ends with a declaration of praise —"Let everything that has breath, praise the Lord!" However, in between Psalm 1 and Psalm 150, there are a lot of ups and downs—victories and battles— times of joy and sorrow—recorded for us to read. The Psalms include a variety of emotions, but throughout the book, praise is the theme.

Our life must be the same. We must have a firm foundation and regardless of what we are facing, let praise be real and genuine and intertwined throughout our journey. Let praise for Him be our theme.

When we have a mindset of praise and a heart of thanksgiving, it keeps our focus on Him and not our problems. When we magnify Him, as Mary did, we are reminded of how great God is and how present He is in our situation. Our problems begin to grow smaller and smaller in comparison to the awesomeness of our God.

Psalm 91 is a beloved passage by many. For generations it has brought comfort to all who read it and know and love God.

He who dwells in the secret place of the Most High shall abide under the shadow of

the Almighty. I will say of the Lord, "*He is* my refuge and my fortress; My God, in Him I will trust." Surely He shall deliver you from the snare of the fowler *And* from the perilous pestilence. He shall cover you with His feathers, And under His wings you shall take refuge; His truth *shall* be your shield and buckler. You shall not be afraid of the terror by night, *Nor* of the arrow *that* flies by day, *Nor* of the pestilence *that* walks in darkness, *Nor* of the destruction *that* lays waste at noonday. A thousand may fall at your side, And ten thousand at your right hand; *But* it shall not come near you. Only with your eyes shall you look, And see the reward of the wicked. Because you have made the Lord, *who* is my refuge, Even the Most High, your dwelling place, No evil shall befall you, Nor shall any plague come near your dwelling; For He shall give His angels charge over you, To keep you in all your ways. In *their* hands they shall bear you up, Lest you dash your foot against a stone. You shall tread upon the lion and the cobra, The young lion and the serpent you shall trample underfoot. "Because he has set his love upon Me, therefore I will deliver him; I will set him on high, because he has known My name. He shall call upon Me, and I will answer him; I *will be* with him in trouble; I will deliver him and honor him. With long life I will satisfy him, And show him My salvation." (vv. 1-16).

PRAISE FOR THE PROMISE

This favorite Psalm reminds us that God has provided a special place for those who love Him to dwell. Our place is a secret haven, hidden from the view of the enemy, safely under His shadow. When I declare, cry out in praise, according to verse two of this psalm that "*He* is my refuge and my fortress; My God, in Him I will trust," I am always comforted by His presence and assurance. By making that declaration I am stepping into the provisions defined in this psalm. Deliverance is promised! Protection is promised! Truth will be my shield! I don't have to be afraid—day or night—of the plot of the enemy. because I have made the Lord my refuge, I have warring angels encamped around me. He promises that because I love Him, He will answer me when I call. He will be with me in trouble. He will honor me and show me His salvation.

Powerful praise is praise that understands and knows God!

Read Psalm 47:6-7. When we sing praises to God with understanding it is powerful. We are focusing and meditating on the greatness and faithfulness of God. *We are blessed as we bless Him!* And those who hear our praises are also.

Sing praises to God, sing praises! Sing praises to our King, sing praises! For God is the King of all the earth; Sing praises with understanding (vv. 6-7).

When we offer praise "with understanding" in our everyday conversations, those who hear know that we have a real relationship and love for God. *Our praise gives them an insight to our revelation knowledge of God.* If they are not saved, it could very well lead to their salvation!

Write a praise offering to God because of Who He is to you without asking Him for anything. In your praise to Him, express truths about God that make you more aware of His sufficiency to meet all your needs:

_____

_____

_____

_____

_____

_____

_____

_____

_____

_____

_____

Read back over what you have just written. What about your own expressions of praise gives you the most comfort and why? What about your praise do you feel would encourage others if they heard it expressed?

_____

_____

PRAISE FOR THE PROMISE

_____

_____

_____

_____

_____

_____

_____

_____

_____

Praise must be priority. It always points to Him, and He is more than enough for whatever we face. He is the answer to everyone's questions. Our praise may be the light that shines in someone's darkness causing them to find their way to Him. No wonder the devil wants you to be silent when it comes to praise!

I love praising God using the written Word. There is something powerful in speaking the unfailing Word of God in the form of praise to Him. His Word is our covenant. It is eternal and unchanging; it strengthens you and encourages you, and the enemy cannot come against it!

Are you going through a trying and difficult time? You feel you are walking according to God's plan but nothing seems to be working out right. Your spirit is heavy and fear has crept in.

Maybe you feel you missed the mark and because of misguided choices, you have created the problems you are facing. So, now the enemy is coming against you with condemnation.

Perhaps you are fighting sickness in your body and you feel hopeless and helpless. The enemy wants you to feel there is nothing that will change your circumstances and he wants to rob you of your joy for life.

The devil wants you to focus on the problems and not the One who is greater than anything you face. He wants to keep your praise silenced. He wants to keep your eyes turned to the battle and not our triumphant King.

When I feel overwhelmed and find my praise becoming lost in my complaining, I pick up the Word of God. I purposefully look for passages that bring comfort and promises recorded in it that encourage me and cause my faith to grow when I read them. Then I turn them into praise.

Let me share an example with you. *Read Isaiah 43:1-2 and Isaiah 53:4-5.*

But now, thus says the Lord, who created you, O Jacob, And He who formed you, O Israel: "Fear not, for I have redeemed you; I have called *you* by your name; You *are* Mine. When you pass through the waters, I *will be* with you; And through the rivers, they shall not overflow you. When you walk through the fire, you shall not be burned, Nor shall the flame scorch you (Isa. 43:1-2).

Surely He has borne our griefs And carried our sorrows; Yet we esteemed Him stricken,

PRAISE FOR THE PROMISE

Smitten by God, and afflicted. But He *was* wounded for our transgressions, He *was* bruised for our iniquities; The chastisement for our peace *was* upon Him, And by His stripes we are healed (Isa. 53:4-5).

Now take words from these two passages and turn them into a praise offering!

"Lord Jesus, I thank You because You created me. I do not have to fear because You have redeemed me. You have called me by name. I am Yours and You are mine and what belongs to You, You will protect! I thank You and praise You because You have assured me that when I pass through this difficult place and feel like I am drowning and am overwhelmed with the cares of this life, I will not be alone, for You are with me. I bless You because the rivers will not overtake me. You will hold back the enemy's plan. Lord, You have assured me through Your Word that when I am going through these fiery trials, I will not be burned or touched by the flames. You are worthy of my praise because You will protect me! I give You praise because You bore my grief and carried my sorrows. I thank You and praise You because You were wounded for my transgressions and bruised for my iniquities. You purchased my peace on Calvary and by Your stripes I am healed! My soul magnifies You because You provided everything I would ever need by dying on the cross. And You defeated every devil in hell when You came forth from the grave! I thank You for You are faithful and will not allow me

*to be destroyed, defeated or distracted. I will keep
praise alive and keep my focus on You. You are more
than enough for me! No weapon formed against me
will prosper—all because of You!"*

*Notice that I didn't ask for anything! I simply gave
genuine heartfelt praise while declaring the truth of
His Word.* At the same time, I encouraged myself by
speaking God's promises that are assured to those
who love Him.

Praying and petitioning God are certainly privileges
bestowed upon the believer, but there is something
powerful about going before the Most High God with
nothing to request, just offering thanks. He is worthy
of our praise!

*The book of Isaiah is special to me. Years ago,
when our sons were young, I was going through a
very dark time in my life. The enemy wanted me to
be lost in depression and discouragement. It was a
difficult and unfamiliar place for me emotionally. In
some ways it seemed even more difficult because I
had no reason or situation to blame it on, but it was
real. I was lost in confusion over how to get "out of
the fog" of depression. I was the same person I had
always been. I was still faithful in church attendance.
I was still teaching Sunday School and going through
the motions of life. My husband and family loved me
and my sons were healthy and happy but the sadness
was real and I hid it from everyone.*

*It was spring, my favorite time of the year. We
lived in a rural community and it was always beautiful
that season. I distinctly remember the day. I could*

PRAISE FOR THE PROMISE

smell the scent of freshly cut grass coming in through the open windows as a gentle breeze was blowing. I could see outside through the big window behind the dining room table where I was sitting. There was a newly born calf standing on wobbly legs just beyond our backyard fence with his protective mom grazing a few feet away. Lavender wisteria wound its way up into the tall pine trees in the edge of the pasture. The azaleas were in full bloom and they were even more vibrant than I remembered from previous springs in their bright hues of pink. The dogwoods were covered in flowers. Hummingbirds were buzzing around their bright red feeders. My sons were playing in their sandbox beside the patio in the backyard. It was an absolutely beautiful day. The sky was a beautiful blue without a cloud in it.

However, my emotions were dark and gray. I didn't understand why.

I was at the dining room table with my Bible open, but not really reading it. My mind was drifting and I was feeling that inexplicable sadness overshadow me again. I remember saying, "God, please I need You." Just then, my two boys, Joel and Jonathan, ages 7 and 3, ran in from their sandbox in the backyard for a drink of water. I had been watching them play from the window. I will always remember what Joel said, "Mom, it must be an early spring for sure, cause the Isaiahs sure are blooming!" He had heard his dad and papaw talking about spring coming earlier than usual that year. I laughed at him calling the azaleas "Isaiahs" and felt a little joy just at the thought of

*his comment. I said, "So, the Isaiahs are blooming?"
He smiled and replied while drinking a cold glass of
water, "They sure are!" And he and his brother ran
back outside to continue playing.*

*And I will never forget what happened next. It was
as if I heard the Lord whisper, "Let Isaiah bloom in
your heart this spring, Rhonda." I can't say I heard
an audible voice, but it was just as clear as if I had.
Sitting right there at my dining room table, I opened
my Bible and began to read passages from Isaiah.
They seemed to jump off the pages at me. I marked
them and I still have that Bible. All these years later,
I will bring that Bible out from time to time and read
those particular passages again and I will remember
with gratitude how it changed me.*

*I read promises and words of hope all recorded
in Isaiah. Promises like: His name is Wonderful,
Counselor, Mighty God, Everlasting Father, Prince
of Peace, and He will keep me in perfect peace and
He will give me a song in the night. I was reminded
that the work of righteousness shall be peace and that
He would make the crooked places straight and the
rough places smooth. I read that my God measured
the waters in the hollow of His hand and that He
calculated the dust of the earth in a measure and
knew the weight of the mountains and hills. I was
reminded that my God never faints or grows weary.
His understanding is unsearchable and He gives
power to the weak and that those who wait on Him
will have renewed strength, they shall run and not
be weary and they shall walk and not faint! He told*

PRAISE FOR THE PROMISE

me through Isaiah that I had nothing to fear because He was holding my hand and would help me. (How amazing is that? The Great God described in this awesome book was still personal enough with me that He held my hand!) I read that the floods and fire would not harm me. And that He would do a new thing! He promised me that He would give me treasures in my darkness and riches in the secret places! He assured me that by His stripes I would be healed. No weapon formed against me would prosper and that my children would also know His peace. I was reminded that His Word would never return void but it would accomplish what He sent it to accomplish. I was reminded that the Spirit of the Lord would comfort those who mourn and give them the garment of praise for the spirit of heaviness!

I began to cry—but these were tears of joy and happiness! I sat at the table and felt God begin to lift that feeling of sorrow and grief. Joy began to return to my spirit!

Isaiah bloomed in my heart that spring!

And I am still grateful all these years later!

I learned a valuable lesson on the power of praise and using the written Word as my guide. When you are lost in grief or worn from the battle and words just don't seem to come out right, pick up your Bible and allow the Spirit of God to lead you and praise Him through His Word. You will be blessed while blessing Him! Your faith will increase and His presence will comfort and strengthen you.

Like Mary, make praise a priority in your life. Praise will bring joy to your heart and His joy will be your strength. Yes, praise is essential in our walk with God.

As you journal this week, search out Scriptures that you can make into a praise offering to God. Write them down and refer back to them often. Look for verses that directly relate to a need in your life or that of a loved one.

When you feel discouraged and the journey seems too great, lift up your head and give Him praise! You will receive renewed revelation of just how amazing He is. It will bring joy to your heart and your joy will give you the strength for the next mile.

Make praise a priority in your daily walk with God. Continual praise for God is another ingredient we need in our vessel.
Praise will cause you to focus on Him and joy will be the result. And as your joy increases, so will your strength for the journey to the promise! Like Mary, regardless of what is ahead, you will be able to say,
"My soul magnifies the Lord and my spirit has rejoiced in God my Savior."

PRAISE FOR THE PROMISE

Week Five

POWER TRUTH

Week Five
POWER TRUTH
Process to the Promise

In our previous lessons, we've talked about ingredients that are beneficial in our journey as we yield to God's purpose: revelation, trust, hope, patience, praise and joy are some we discussed. Mix a dedicated and faithful mentor in to help us keep it all together and we have the right combination for a successful "recipe" in the making.

Those are the sweet and good ingredients in our vessel!

But then there are those ingredients we would rather skip! The bitter ingredient that comes from the pain of rejection, the sour ingredient that is so hard to take when you are disappointed or confused by unexpected events and circumstances—those ingredients are a source of frustration and hurt, but His grace is present and His strength will enable you to endure.

We are assured the end results will be worth the hardships and trials we may endure for a season. We must focus on His promise and not the pain, fully aware this too shall pass and He will be faithful to His Word.

Ye are of God, little children, and have overcome them: because greater is he that is in you, than he that is in the world (1 John 4:4 KJV).

Week Five

PROCESS TO THE PROMISE

Week Five
PROCESS TO THE PROMISE
LUKE 2:1-6

Throughout this study, we have discussed the importance of yielding our vessels to God. As committed believers and followers of Jesus Christ, we desire to please Him and live a life of service to Him. Our love for Him causes us to want to disciple other followers and win the lost for the Kingdom of God.

We are aware that God needs laborers in the
vineyard. The harvest is great and God desires
for us to reach out and bring them in.
He also wants us to encourage fellow
believers and disciple converts.

We truly want to be a yielded vessel, clean, accessible, and trusting God throughout this journey. We want to be among those who are willing and able to endure the heat when necessary. We desire to be a vessel of honor for Him.

We have talked about the importance of laying down reasoning and walking in revelation. We have discussed the value of a true mentor and friend to agree with us in faith, while recognizing that there are times when we are the mentor someone needs. We discussed the value of total trust and how genuine trust births hope and true hope births patience. Trust, hope and patience are key ingredients that help us walk out God's plan to fruition in our life. Last week's lesson was about the value of praise and the role it plays in our faith walk. A heart of praise continually to God will help us keep our focus on Him rather than the storms and trials that we experience along the way. Praise helps us to be joyful even in the midst of hard times and the joy of the Lord is our strength!

There are many people of faith in the Word that gave us examples of being a yielded vessel of honor for God, but Mary's story is a fascinating one. All in one glorious evening, there was an amazing proclamation given to her concerning the promised Messiah. Gabriel appeared to her and she was chosen with the great honor of being the mother of the Son of God. Mary willingly yielded her vessel to the purpose and plan of God. God, through Gabriel, shared the news of Elizabeth's miracle conception of her own son to Mary that same night. Mary's heart was overjoyed! She could hardly contain the news of what had happened with Elizabeth and what was proclaimed to happen in her own life.

Mary left as soon as possible to meet Elizabeth and received the confirmation of what the angel had spoken. Mary heard the prophecy and blessing of Elizabeth and they rejoiced together. Mary praised God in advance of those things promised her because she believed in her heart and knew that God would perform what He said He would. She would stay with Elizabeth for three months. Elizabeth was that friend and mentor during that time and, no doubt, spoke

PROCESS TO THE PROMISE

encouragement to Mary for the days that would follow their time together.

The days ahead would be uncertain. Mary would need reassurance. Yes, the journey for Mary began the night Gabriel appeared. The process to her promise had begun!

But, imagine what it may have been like for Mary after her time with Elizabeth. I imagine that it could have been like this…

Mary was home in Nazareth now. It had been months since her time at Elizabeth's house. Word of Mary's condition had begun to spread. Many doubted her—most, in fact. Some voiced it. Others were silent. But Mary knew their heart. Some would look the other way when she walked by. Others would whisper and glare at her and some friends she had known her whole life wouldn't even acknowledge her presence. Even some family rejected her. Then there were those who really wanted to believe her but just couldn't seem to grasp that she would be the mother of their long awaited Messiah. There was bickering between those who doubted and those who believed. Mary grieved as she felt she was the source of conflict with her family and friends. She truly felt alone in a crowd and the pain of rejection was deep.

Joseph had experienced it, too. Mary thanked God often for Joseph. She thanked God for the revelation he had been given and for his faith to receive it. She couldn't imagine what it would have been like for her had Joseph forsaken her too.

Pots, Pans & PROPHECIES

The days seemed endless but yet they seemed to move at a rapid pace all at the same time. Mary cherished her sweet time with Elizabeth. Elizabeth had poured into her spirit and given her words of encouragement, and those words were of great worth now. Mary pondered them often. She remembered fondly what Elizabeth had said that first day she went to her, "Blessed is she who believed, for there will be a fulfillment of those things which were told her from the Lord." Mary's heart rejoiced that God called her blessed for believing by faith what she had been told by Gabriel.

Yes, Mary trusted God. She loved Him and knew her experience was real. No one would ever take that from her. She knew that one day all would know what she spoke was truth, but this time, the waiting, the time between the proclamation and the promise, these were hard and lonely days.

Mary knew the prophecies concerning the birth of the Messiah. She certainly had made herself more familiar with them since Gabriel's announcement! She knew her Son would be born in the City of David, in Bethlehem. She didn't know how that would happen, but she couldn't concern herself with the details. God would take care of it all. She knew that in her heart. She and Joseph had believed God and willingly yielded to His plan and there were no regrets. None!

But still, if she thought too long and hard about it all, fear would begin to plague her and trouble her spirit. So she wouldn't dwell on the unknown. No, she

PROCESS TO THE PROMISE

purposed instead to hold the revelation she had been given close to her heart.

Mary was absolutely certain that God, who had done the impossible for her and for Elizabeth, would certainly take care of all that concerned her.

He would work out every detail. She had no doubt!

When you read of Mary's dedication, perhaps you feel you can relate and you rejoice because your determination is strong and your revelation is still very real and in the forefront of your mind. You are as determined as ever that you will continually walk as that vessel of honor for God and you are excited and joyful at what lies ahead for you.

Or perhaps that is not the case. If you are completely honest with yourself, maybe you have found your determination weakening and you can't see clearly the revelation you once had from God. You are trying to hide it from those around you, but it is becoming increasingly more difficult.

When you purposed in your heart to follow wholeheartedly after God, it was at a time when you felt closest to Him. His presence was real and you were stirred in your heart. Making a commitment to yield to His will may have seemed almost easy at that point. You were excited about your decision, and the words of prophecy that would confirm your calling and your plans to follow God just added to your anticipation.

But then life, everyday life, and its routines set in. The unexpected interruptions that get you off track from accomplishing your goals seem almost

commonplace. The joy of yielding to His plan that had been yours in the beginning is now fading in the face of everyday responsibilities.

Excitement and anticipation for what is ahead seem to be slowly turning to frustration and uncertainty. You have begun to question your choice to give your life totally in service to God. After all, you can certainly be a Christian without giving so much of your time and service. You can easily think of a long list of others who are less involved and committed in their walk with Him, and they seem content and fine with that! *So why aren't you?*

Perhaps you have found yourself reasoning away your revelation and your desire to walk in your purpose is waning as you give yourself a list of valid reasons why you can't, not yet anyway, totally sell out to God's plan.

> *Is that where you find yourself? Are you there? Have you found yourself becoming weary in well doing? Your strength, and even your desire to continue, seem weaker by the day. You feel like one more battle, one more attack from the enemy will push you over the edge.*

Don't stay in that mindset! Remember how you felt when you first made yourself accessible to God. Like Mary, you must purpose to hold on to the revelation and allow your joy to return!

Based on our study so far, what do you think are some things that will help you get out of the mindset of defeat? Take a moment and write down your thoughts.

_____

_____

_____

_____

_____

_____

_____

_____

_____

_____

_____

*Remember: Revelation knowledge of God
leads to trust in Him. Trust births hope. Hope
brings forth patience. Praise helps keep your
focus on God and restores your joy. And a
good friend and mentor will help you hold on
to these things!*

God knew you would face uncertainty. He knew the enemy would try and bring you to a place of reasoning and cause you to let go of your revelation. That has been his strategy for generations. The enemy desires to build that stronghold in your mind so you will feel overwhelmed and give in. He wants you to

feel like a failure and weigh you down with the cares of this life.

You may be saying in your heart, "It's easier said than done to hold on at this point. You don't know what I am facing."

Remember, we all have battles and we all face the opposition of the enemy, *especially when we are going in the right direction!* But God will not leave us powerless in the face of our enemy. He will never leave us defenseless against our foe.

Let's go back again to the very beginning of our study and think about this once more:

In God's house there are many vessels with many purposes. We are those vessels! Like the pots and pans we use in our kitchens, as God's chosen vessels, we must be:

- *Clean*
- *Accessible*
- *Willing to take the ingredients*
- *And able to endure the heat*

Or, the mission will not be accomplished through us!

When we feel like quitting, or lose our enthusiasm for ministry or service, often it is because some of the ingredients are hard to take or we have entered the "heat of the oven."

One of my favorite recipes contains a variety of ingredients. It has apples, flour, sugar, cinnamon, and lemon juice in the required list. The apples are delicious. However, flour when uncooked is bland and tasteless. Sugar is sweet. Cinnamon is terribly bitter alone and lemon juice is sour! However, together,

PROCESS TO THE PROMISE

mixed correctly with the right measurements of each, placed in the proper, clean and accessible vessel— after enduring the heat—a delicious (I am so serious when I say that!) apple cobbler is produced. Top it with a scoop of vanilla ice cream and everybody is happy! Say amen!

We've talked about ingredients that are beneficial in our journey as we yield to God's purpose: Revelation, trust, hope, patience, praise, and joy are some we discussed. Mix a dedicated and faithful mentor in to help us keep it all together and we have the makings of a successful "recipe" in the works. Those are the sweet and good ingredients in our vessel.

What about the bitter ingredients we weren't expecting?

That sour ingredient that just seemed unfair was added to it all, and all the bland "nothing spiritually profound happening" days that just seem endless thrown in the equation. All these are added to the mix of things in life and it seems so complicated at times.

To top it all off, now the fiery trial that was totally unexpected comes into action.

We must remember what the Word says and what we have discussed in the previous lessons. God will enable us to endure and we will come forth victoriously. We cannot give up just before our greatest victory! We cannot walk away from our calling or purpose and abort the fulfillment of the plan and purpose God has designed for us.

Let's read 1 Peter 1:3-7:

Praise God, the Father of our Lord Jesus Christ. God is so good, and by raising Jesus from death, he has given us new life and a hope that lives on. God has something stored up for you in heaven, where it will never decay or be ruined or disappear. You have faith in God, whose power will protect you until the last day. Then he will save you, just as he has always planned to do. On that day you will be glad, even if you have to go through many hard trials for a while. Your faith will be like gold that has been tested in a fire. And these trials will prove that your faith is worth much more than gold that can be destroyed. They will show that you will be given praise and honour and glory when Jesus Christ returns (CEV).

These powerful verses tell us that God has provided new life and given eternal rewards and a lasting hope for those who are His. Great things await us in Heaven that will never be ruined or destroyed.

If we continue to hold to our faith in Him, His power will be with us and protect us until the very end, no matter what fiery trials we may face. He will bring us through! Nothing will take our joy. The trials we face will prove that our faith cannot be destroyed by the enemy. It will come forth as pure gold and worth much more and God promises that He will reward us openly.

PROCESS TO THE PROMISE

We all love Romans 8. We referred to a portion of it in week three's lesson. This chapter in Paul's letter to the Romans begins by reminding us that there is no condemnation to those who are in Christ. It concludes assuring us that nothing can separate us from the love of God which is in Christ Jesus. It begins with "no condemnation" and ends with "no separation" for the believer!

But right in the middle of this amazing chapter, Paul reminds us that there are sufferings in this present time. *Read Romans 8:17-18.*

> And if children, then heirs; heirs of God, and joint-heirs with Christ; if so be that we suffer with him, that we may be also glorified together. For I reckon that the sufferings of this present time are not worthy to be compared with the glory which shall be revealed in us (KJV).

Read it closely again and rejoice. Yes, take joy in this promise! Even though it reminds us that there will be suffering in this life, we are assured that the sufferings here are not worthy to be compared with the glory which shall be revealed in us.

We are His children and heirs of God—joint-heirs with Jesus. We may suffer for the cause of Christ for a season. We may suffer in the battles of this life for a time. We may endure heat and know grief, but we will be rewarded beyond our ability to comprehend for our faithfulness to Him in our times of trials.

Read more of Paul's words found in 2 Corinthians 4:17-18:

For our light and momentary troubles are achieving for us an eternal glory that far outweighs them all. So we fix our eyes not on what is seen, but on what is unseen, since what is seen is temporary, but what is unseen is eternal (NIV).

How can Paul call his troubles "light and momentary" when he has suffered so much for the cause of Christ? In 2 Corinthians 11:23-28 (AB) Paul gives an account of some of the things he endured and suffered. Among them are extensive and abundant labors, multiple imprisonments, and beatings with countless stripes and frequently to the point of death. Five times the Jews beat him with 39 stripes, three times he was beaten with rods and once even stoned. Three times he was shipwrecked at sea. Many times he was on treacherous journeys and experienced perils from rivers and bandits, from the Jews, and from the Gentiles. He experienced perils in the city, in the desert places, and in the sea. He experienced perils from those posing as believers, in toils and hardships, sleepless nights, hunger and thirst, cold and exposure, and lack of clothing. Along with all of that, he could never get away from his daily inescapable pressure of his care and anxiety of all the churches. *Even still he called these sufferings light and momentary troubles!*

PROCESS TO THE PROMISE

I believe he called them "light and momentary" because of the contrast in comparison to the greatness of our rewards for enduring our trials with faith. He experienced a glimpse into the rewards that would be ours for our faithfulness to God in this life. Paul was confident, even after all he experienced, to say that none of what he suffered was even worthy to be compared to the glory that would be revealed in us.

Paul declared with confidence that the troubles we endure are achieving for us an eternal glory that *far outweighs* them all!

Therefore, Paul said for us to "fix our eyes not on what is seen, but on what is unseen, since what is seen is temporary, but what is unseen is eternal." He was saying to look beyond the moment. Don't look at the temporary trials, battles, struggles, and heartaches for these shall pass! Look to what we can see in the spirit by faith for those things are eternal.

What about these verses in Paul's writing brought you comfort and hope? Write a praise offering using the content of Romans 8:17-18 and 2 Corinthians 4:17-18:

_____

_____

_____

_____

_____

_____

_____

_____

_____

Remember, this too shall pass. Rejoice! Difficult times are temporary. God is mindful of you every moment of every day and He will take care of you. He will work out details and order your steps. He will open the right doors and shut the wrong ones. He knows exactly where you are and He will reward you for your faithfulness!

Read Psalm 139:1-3:

O Jehovah, thou hast searched me, and known me. Thou knowest my downsitting and mine uprising; Thou understandest my thought afar off. Thou searchest out my path and my lying down, and art acquainted with all my ways (ASV).

In your own thoughts about this verse, express why this is a comforting passage to you personally:

_____

_____

_____

_____

_____

_____

_____

Look back to Mary's story. She had willingly by faith begun a journey marked with uncertainty, but she trusted God with the details. The process to the promise had not been easy and now she was on the

PROCESS TO THE PROMISE

way to the performance of the promise. Yet still the fiery trials were not over. *Look at Luke 2:1-6.*

> And it came to pass in those days, that there went out a decree from Caesar Augustus, that all the world should be taxed. (And this taxing was first made when Cyrenius was governor of Syria.) And all went to be taxed, every one into his own city. And Joseph also went up from Galilee, out of the city of Nazareth, into Judaea, unto the city of David, which is called Bethlehem; (because he was of the house and lineage of David:) To be taxed with Mary his espoused wife, being great with child. And so it was, that, while they were there, the days were accomplished that she should be delivered (KJV).

Notice in Luke 2:1 that a phrase we all like is used: "It came to pass!" This time of trials will come to pass and you can trust God with the details like Mary did. Caesar Augustus thought he had an idea to tax the whole known world but I believe God used him to get Mary and Joseph in the right place at the right time for Jesus to be born. God had a man move the whole world to get one obedient couple in their appointed place and *He will do the same for you* if necessary when you walk in obedience to Him! God will move obstacles and do the impossible for you when you yield to His purpose. He just needs willing vessels. The details He can and will handle.

A Point to Ponder: It is interesting to me that "all went to be taxed, everyone to his own city." Everyone went to their city based on their family's lineage. Have you ever thought about it like this? That means that there were people Mary and Joseph would have known in Bethlehem. Family members were there with them, yet not one person would give up their room for Mary. She was obviously about to give birth. Joseph sought for a place for her to rest but there was no room in the inn. Not one person in the family, not one close or distant relative was willing to give Mary a place to rest. Sometimes those we love the most are the ones who understand the least the call of God on our lives. Rejection from them hurts the most but remain faithful. God will reveal to all in time that His hand is on you and His purpose for you is good!

Luke 2:6 declares that while they were there "the days were accomplished." The wait had ended. Victory was *now* and all their—friends, family and strangers—would soon hear of the glorious and miraculous birth. *Your wait will soon end!* The days of your trial will soon be accomplished and all will know God's favor is on your life.

> *Lift up your head and rejoice! The best could be just ahead! Good things are coming! For He is faithful that promised!*

PROCESS TO THE PROMISE

Yes, you will experience some unpleasant places in your journey to the promise. Bitter and unpleasant ingredients will come, but He has equipped you with the good ingredients that will overcome those painful ones. You are stronger than you realize.

The same Holy Spirit that made all things possible with Mary in Luke 1:35 will also come and equip you for the task that is in front of you. You are empowered by Him to accomplish all that God is calling you to do.

Read Acts 1:8 and 1 John 4.4:

But you will receive power when the Holy Spirit comes on you; and you will be my witnesses in Jerusalem, and in all Judea and Samaria, and to the ends of the earth" (Acts 1:8 NIV).

Ye are of God, little children, and have overcome them: because greater is he that is in you, than he that is in the world (1 John 4:4 KJV).

The enabling power of the Spirit of God will strengthen you through the place of testing and trials. The heat of the battle is temporary. What will be produced through your vessel as a result of your faithfulness and willingness to endure will be worth it all. The Word of God is in you and your faith will prevail.

It is through the Word of God dwelling in common vessels like us, that strongholds in the kingdom

of darkness are brought down, that powers and principalities are put under our feet, and that great and mighty works for God are accomplished in these last days. The sick will be healed, the spiritually destitute will receive life eternal, fallen man will be restored to God, and the devils of Hell will tremble at the power that is working in you and through you!

Don't underestimate what God desires to birth through you. Much will be accomplished because your vessel was clean, accessible and endured the heat for a season.

Endure the process to the promise. The performance of it is coming and the wait will be worth it all!

PROCESS TO THE PROMISE

Week Six

POWER TRUTH

Week Six
POWER TRUTH
Performance of the Promise

In our final lesson of *Pots, Pans & Prophecies*, we will rejoice together as we reflect on the joy Mary experienced in the fulfillment of God's promise for her life.

We will be comforted as we are reminded that our faith in God is the "confirmation, the title deed" of the things we hope for.

The promise is worth the process! The wait is worth it!

We will renew our determination to remain a faithful vessel of honor for Him as we journey here, assured that His reward for our faithfulness is evident in this life and guaranteed in the life to come.

Let us hold fast the confession of *our* hope without wavering, for He who promised is faithful (Heb. 10:23).

Week Six

PERFORMANCE OF THE PROMISE

Week Six
PERFORMANCE OF THE PROMISE
Luke 2:7-20

In last week's lesson, we read in Luke 2:6 that Mary's "days were completed for her to be delivered." In your spiritual walk with God, those words cause joy and happiness. Yes, the days are completed and your deliverance has come! These are words we all want to hear.

This week, we will rejoice at the assurance of promises fulfilled. The time between the proclamation and the performance can be long, lonely, and overwhelming at times, but the performance of all you have waited for makes the journey, even though perilous at times, worth every step! There is satisfaction in obedience to God, even before the battles cease. The peace of knowing you are walking in agreement with your Creator brings contentment even before those things you have hoped come to fruition.

We have discussed the need for trust, hope, and patience in our walk with God. Those ingredients bring inexplicable calm to the heart of the believer, even in the waiting time.

In Luke 2:7-20, the long awaited Promise for Mary arrived! Her journey had been amazing. She had known of God's miraculous power to do the impossible. She had known the joy of complete surrender and the promise of blessings untold that would result from her obedience. She had held tightly to Elizabeth's pronouncement of blessings on her for her faith in God. She knew God would bring forth exactly what He had spoken. However, even in her anticipation and assurance of the great things to come, she had experienced many hurtful and painful battles in the process.

But now she was here! The painful place was behind her! The Promise had come!

And she brought forth her firstborn Son, and wrapped Him in swaddling cloths, and laid Him in a manger, because there was no room for them in the inn. Now there were in the same country shepherds living out in the fields, keeping watch over their flock by night. And behold, an angel of the Lord stood before them, and the glory of the Lord shone around them, and they were greatly afraid. Then the angel said to them, "Do not be afraid, for behold, I bring you good tidings of great joy which will be to all people. For there is born to you this day in the city of David a Savior, who is Christ the Lord. And this *will be* the sign to you: You will find a Babe wrapped in swaddling cloths, lying in a manger" (Luke 2:7-12).

So it was, when the angels had gone away from them into heaven, that the shepherds said to one another, "Let us now go to Bethlehem and

PERFORMANCE OF THE PROMISE

see this thing that has come to pass, which the Lord has made known to us." And they came with haste and found Mary and Joseph, and the Babe lying in a manger. Now when they had seen *Him*, they made widely known the saying which was told them concerning this Child. And all those who heard *it* marveled at those things which were told them by the shepherds. But Mary kept all these things and pondered *them* in her heart. Then the shepherds returned, glorifying and praising God for all the things that they had heard and seen, as it was told them (Luke 2:15-20).

Imagine the joy in Mary's heart as a result of the turn of events in her life that night! In my imagination, it could have been like this:

The day had certainly started differently than it would end! Mary and Joseph had made the required journey to Bethlehem. Along the way, they had passed many familiar faces as they traveled. She had again experienced the pain of rejection from some she knew. No one had given them a place to rest. No one was willing to be inconvenienced for Mary, not even being aware she was about to give birth.

Joseph had done the best he could. He found a place for them to find rest because there was no room in the inn. It was not what either of them planned or expected but it was sufficient. The best part for Mary was that she could be alone, away from the

crowd that had gathered as a result of the decree of the census.

Then, everything began to happen so quickly, and now the wait was over. The Promised One had come and the joy that flooded her heart was like nothing she had ever known before!

Mary was embracing her firstborn Son. The Messiah had come—but so had her Baby! She held Him close and listened to the sweet sounds He made as He cooed in her arms. She wrapped Him snuggly and tenderly kissed His face. I imagine, like any new mother, she would have said, "What beautiful eyes! Look at His hair! What curls He has already, Joseph! Is that a dimple? He's perfectly and amazingly wonderful! What a precious gift! What a fine young Man He will be! Dear One, Your Name is Jesus and what a lovely Name it is! What a wonderful Name it will be to many, my sweet Son."

The presence of God filled the place. After all, God certainly would be in attendance for the birth of His Only Begotten Son.

And not far from them, in the fields nearby, shepherds were watching their flocks in the night. It seemed like any other night on the job for them. It was an ordinary evening with ordinary people doing ordinary things, but all the ordinary was about to become extraordinary, and that night would forever change the lives of all who received the news about to be given!

All in that moment, Heaven seemed to open. The light above was shining like the sun. Ordinary people

PERFORMANCE OF THE PROMISE

stopped doing ordinary things. Everyone's routine seemed unimportant. Everyone's focus changed in a moment's time. For the first gospel message was about to be preached by an angel. Attention was demanded. Those in attendance would hear the sermon.

The sky was reflecting the glorious light of truth that had entered the world. Darkness fled the scene as if it knew it could not abide in the presence of the declaration about to be proclaimed. Yes, the Good News was about to be declared!

For God's plan to restore fallen man was born that very night!

It was a short sermon the angel delivered, but the message was powerful. It brought redemptive, revelation knowledge to its audience The angel declared, "Do not be afraid, for behold, I bring you good tidings of great joy which will be to all people. For there is born to you this day in the city of David, a Savior, who is Christ the Lord. And this will be a sign to you: You will find a Babe wrapped in swaddling clothes, lying in a manger."

Suddenly the sky filled with angels—a whole host of them—and they declared together with great joy and confidence: "Glory to God in the highest and on earth, peace goodwill toward men!"

Revelation requires a response and great revelation removes reservation! The shepherds said immediately to each other, "Let us go now!" They said, "…and see this thing that has come to pass, which the Lord made known to us." There was no

Pots, Pans & PROPHECIES

doubt in them. When you have revelation knowledge, no one can take it from you.

The shepherds hurriedly made their way to Mary and Joseph and Baby Jesus. They found them just like they were told they would.

I can imagine the joy in their hearts and in their words to Mary and Joseph as they shared the story of the angelic visitation. No doubt, Mary and Joseph would have shared their encounters with them. Everyone's faith was strengthened as they encouraged each other with the revelation they had been given.

This visit to Mary and her newborn Son by the shepherds was better than being in a luxurious setting, attended by a host of her family and friends.

For this visitation was another sign of confirmation.

Mary didn't need an angel that night for she was embracing the Son of God!

I am convinced the night her Promise came that not once did Mary reflect on her painful journey that brought her here. No, not that night! Not once did she cry in her sorrow for what she had endured. The words "Why me? Why did I have to go through all I did to get to this place?" were not thought, much less were they spoken.

No, quite the opposite was taking place! Every tear, every sorrow, every battle, every pain waned in comparison to the glorious manifestation of the Promise. Every sacrifice, every fear and every dread

PERFORMANCE OF THE PROMISE

faded into nothingness in the face of the Promised One!

Yes, it was worth it all. All! She would do it all again to experience the joy of that night. Her obedience was greatly rewarded. God had blessed beyond measure. Yes, a thousand times and beyond, a resounding yes! It was worth it all.

The shepherds could not contain what they had been told and witnessed. They spread the news quickly. No doubt those in the inn who would not give up their room heard the news. No doubt family members and those who knew them heard of the miraculous events that transpired in Bethlehem. Strangers were hearing of this couple from Nazareth who had yielded to God's plan and as a result the whole world would be forever changed.

One willing vessel, one obedient child of God made a difference!

And Mary, well, she pondered all these things in her heart. She meditated on every event and etched them into her memory. She would never forget and no one would ever take from her the incredible memories that were made that night.

The untold joys of her obedience could not be measured and she would continue to walk in submission to God's plan every day of her life—without one single regret.

Glory to God in the highest! For He makes all things beautiful in His time!

Write a prayer of thanksgiving for the performance of your promise. You may still be waiting, but by faith, see those things that are coming and rejoice because He is faithful and it will come to pass.

_____
_____
_____
_____
_____
_____
_____
_____
_____
_____

Yes, this life is a walk of faith. We are all in different places in our walk of obedience. Some are on the mountaintop experiencing victory. Some are in the valley, holding on to hope that "this too shall pass." Others feel they are experiencing nothing of any magnitude, good or bad, and are fighting to keep from growing complacent.

Regardless of our place at the moment, *we must be determined to go forward* with the assurance that all is well, looking beyond what we see to what we cannot see in the natural.

Let's look to a familiar and loved passage that defines our faith:

PERFORMANCE OF THE PROMISE

Now faith is the substance of things hoped for, the evidence of things not seen (Heb. 11:1 KJV).

Read it again in the Amplified Version.

Now faith is the assurance (the confirmation, the title deed) of the things [we] hope for, being the proof of things [we] do not see *and* the conviction of their reality [faith perceiving as real fact what is not revealed to the senses] (AB).

Faith is the "confirmation, the title deed" of the things we hope for! If I hold the title deed, I own the property identified on that deed. Faith is the proof of things we do not see but know in our hearts are a reality.

Faith is evidence! Evidence is a strong word. It substantiates one's claims. Evidence in a court of law will convince a jury of either guilt or innocence. Faith is proof we have received what we are believing God for—even though it has not yet been fulfilled.

As I prayed about this final lesson, I felt directed to look to the Word for promises that are there for us. My prayer is that this will cause us to reflect on the promises that are ours as a result of our obedience. I pray that reading again some of the assurances in the Word will reassure us that the process is worth it. Like Mary, we will have no regrets when we obtain what we have waited patiently for in faith.

Our love for God is our motivation to serve Him but God is so good to us. A life of obedience, He will reward. He assures us that if we love Him, know His Word, and live according to it, He will bless us!

Read the following passages carefully. As you read these verses, look at the importance of abiding in the Word of God and the results of it.

If ye abide in me, and my words abide in you, ask whatsoever ye will, and it shall be done unto you (John 15:7 ASV).

Let the message of Christ dwell among you richly as you teach and admonish one another with all wisdom through psalms, hymns and songs from the Spirit, singing to God with gratitude in your hearts. And whatever you do, whether in word or deed, do it all in the name of the Lord Jesus, giving thanks to God the Father through him (Col. 3:16-17 NIV).

I write to you, fathers, because you have known him who is from the beginning. I write to you, young men, because you are strong, and the word of God lives in you, and you have overcome the evil one. Do not love the world or anything in the world. If anyone loves the world, the love of the Father is not in him. For everything in the world—the cravings of sinful man, the lust of his eyes and the boasting of what he has and does—comes not from the

PERFORMANCE OF THE PROMISE

Father but from the world. The world and its desires pass away, but the man who does the will of God lives forever (1 John 2:14-17 NIV 1984).

I have hidden your word in my heart that I might not sin against you (Ps. 119:11 NIV).

Write your thoughts concerning what you read. What do you see resulting in the life of a believer because of the Word being "in them" and applied to their thoughts and actions?

_____

_____

_____

_____

_____

_____

_____

_____

_____

_____

_____

_____

_____

_____

_____

The Word of God keeps that necessary
ingredient of revelation knowledge alive
and well in our vessel. The Word of God is
essential for our victory!

It is so important that we are honest with ourselves concerning our thoughts. Our thoughts can either increase our faith or break it down. Our thoughts must be based on the Word of God and the revelation of Him through His Word.

The enemy is afraid of your purpose! He wants to keep you off track and delay the promise God has planned for you. He hates it when you focus on the truth of the Word. He cannot alter truth. Lies—no matter how many are told—do not change the absolute truth. When you know the Word, you recognize his lies. You stand on the Word—the truth—without compromising, and it strengthens you to endure till the end in confident and absolute faith!

Let's consider some ways the enemy comes with distractions in the minds and hearts of a believer. We discussed earlier John 10:10. The enemy's agenda is short and to the point. It is found in this verse. He comes to kill, steal and destroy. He wants to kill your dreams, steal your hope and destroy you and your promise. He is successful only if we allow him in our minds through suggestions.

Think about the following examples of the enemy's strategy to distract from the Word and its promises to the follower of Christ. Then look at just one promise of Scripture— just one of many—that counteracts his lies and suggestions.

PERFORMANCE OF THE PROMISE

Perhaps you are a minister or a pastor's wife and you feel you have labored faithfully and had little success in bringing in a harvest. You have questioned your decision to be where you are at this point in your life. You don't know if you can wait much longer. The enemy wants you to quit or move on. He doesn't want you to reap in the field where you have planted seeds of truth. He wants to rob you of your harvest but claim the promise in *Galatians 6:9*!

> And let us not lose heart *and* grow weary *and* faint in acting nobly *and* doing right, for in due time *and* at the appointed season we shall reap, if we do not loosen *and* relax our courage *and* faint (AB).

Your harvest is coming!

Some of you are battling physical problems. You are tired from the struggle and are trying to stay positive in your thinking and in your outlook on life, but it is increasingly more difficult. It is hard for you to think of being productive in your walk with God; you feel limited in what you can do because of sickness or pain. Reach out in faith and hold to the promise in *Isaiah 53:5*.

> But He was wounded for our transgressions, He was bruised for our guilt *and* iniquities; the chastisement [needful to obtain] peace *and* well-being for us was upon Him, and with the

stripes [that wounded] Him we are healed *and* made whole (AB).

Your healing is coming!

Maybe you have lost your job or your finances have been drastically cut, and you live in fear of how you will provide for your family. You try to dismiss the dread of the unknown. But with every passing day, the bills are still there and you wonder if you will ever be able to dig your way out. You certainly can't afford to focus more on your calling and purpose until you get yourself back on track financially—or at least that's what the enemy would like for you to think. Dismiss his suggestions of defeat by claiming *Philippians 4:19.*

And my God shall supply all your need according to His riches in glory by Christ Jesus.

Your provision is coming!

Or perhaps you have a rebellious son or daughter. Your heart breaks as they walk away, continually it seems, from the truth you have instilled in them. You are crushed and they seem oblivious to your pain. You have mentored others and your own children won't receive instruction. You fear for them as their choices bring one problem after another for them to face. How bad will it have to get for them before they wake up? You lose sleep and dread the next phone

PERFORMANCE OF THE PROMISE

call for fear it is more bad news concerning your son or daughter. Proclaim the promises found in *Isaiah 54:13*! Declare these words over your family, "My children will be taught by the Lord and great shall be their peace! Yes, as for me and my house we will serve the Lord!"

> All your children *shall* be taught by the Lord,
> And great *shall* be the peace of your children.

Your prodigal is coming!

You have ministered to others, encouraging them when they were discouraged and disheartened. Now you feel alone in the battle. You are secretly struggling with fear and you feel your trust in God is failing. You don't want anyone to know that you are battling discouragement. Your strength is gone and so is your joy. Remember the truth recorded in *Isaiah 12:2-3*. The Lord is your salvation and strength! You will find trust again. And the joy of your salvation will return.

> Behold, God, my salvation! I will trust and not be afraid, for the Lord God is my strength and song; yes, He has become my salvation. Therefore with joy will you draw water from the wells of salvation (AB).

Your strength is coming!

Pots, Pans & PROPHECIES

Perhaps you have walked in an anointing and you have known the joy of serving God. Now you feel as if you are going through the motions and your words feel empty when you speak them. You are still seeing results when you minister, but you leave feeling empty instead of refreshed. You almost feel hypocritical at times. Your words are saying one thing and you mean what you're saying, but your heart feels void. You hunger to be touched with a fresh move of His Spirit. You don't feel like you have the strength to take one more step. Read *Isaiah 40:31* and praise God, remembering His faithfulness, for He will bring renewal and restore your strength. You will be revived and empowered again!

> But those who wait for the Lord [who expect, look for, and hope in Him] shall change *and* renew their strength *and* power; they shall lift their wings *and* mount up [close to God] as eagles [mount up to the sun]; they shall run and not be weary, they shall walk and not faint *or* become tired (AB).

Your revival is coming!

Maybe you are fearful and have lost your peace. You can't seem to get your thoughts together for being distracted from the emotional drain you are constantly faced with. Something has got to change. Your heart is troubled and your peace is gone. Read

PERFORMANCE OF THE PROMISE

John 14:27 and rejoice because He gave you His peace and His peace is perfect!

> Peace I leave with you; my peace I give you. I do not give to you as the world gives. Do not let your hearts be troubled and do not be afraid (NIV).

Your peace is coming!

Take a few moments and write down a Scripture that you feel is a promise you need to hold on to at this time in your life. Then read over it several times and ask God to allow that promise to take root in your heart. Thank Him for giving you the promise in His eternal, unchanging Word.

_____

_____

_____

_____

_____

_____

_____

_____

As His children, we must continually remember what God has spoken and what He has promised. We willingly give our lives in service to Him so that others may know Him. It is a privilege to walk in covenant with Him, and He blesses those who are faithful.

Pots, Pans & PROPHECIES

Read Galatians 2:20.

I have been crucified with Christ; it is no longer I who live, but Christ lives in me; and the *life* which I now live in the flesh I live by faith in the Son of God, who loved me and gave Himself for me.

In your own words, write down what you feel Galatians 2:20 means to you as you purpose to live as a vessel of honor for God.

_____

_____

_____

_____

_____

_____

_____

_____

As we bring our study to a close, I pray you have renewed your commitment to walk daily as a vessel of honor. Hold diligently to your revelation knowledge of God. Trust Him and allow that trust to keep hope alive in your heart. Hope will bring forth patience. Hope is not something a believer does, it is something a believer has! When you truly grasp that hope, you will wait for the promise in confident patience.

You will receive your promise, for those who live a life of obedience are blessed while being a blessing.

PERFORMANCE OF THE PROMISE

Do all you can for Him. Make every day
count for Christ. And never lose sight of your
promise. It is on the way. Because He
is faithful that promised!

Let us hold fast the confession of *our* hope
without wavering, for He who promised is
faithful (Heb. 10:23).

God will open the doors that He wants opened
in your life. He will shut the ones that will lead to
heartache or destruction. He will answer your
prayers and order your steps. He is mindful of you
and knows you have been faithful. No good thing you
have done will go unrewarded. God will answer your
prayers and reward you openly. For every battle you
have fought in His name, you will find victory.

Don't give up! Your promise is coming!

One ordinary day, when you are doing ordinary
things, the light from heaven will shine and dispel
your darkness. In one moment's time, it will all turn
around. No, don't give up!

Your promise is coming! And it may be today!

Don't be afraid, you don't have to fear. For unto
you a Savior was born!

Mary embraced her Promise, She held the Son
of God that amazing night. Your promise is coming!
And the Son of God is embracing you while you wait.
He will not leave you or forsake you and He is faithful
to His Word.

The rewards of living as a yielded vessel for Him are great, not only in the life to come, but in this life as well.

So always be clean, accessible, willing and able to take the heat and something amazing will be birthed through you! Many will be blessed because of your obedience!

PERFORMANCE OF THE PROMISE

Pots, Pans & PROPHECIES

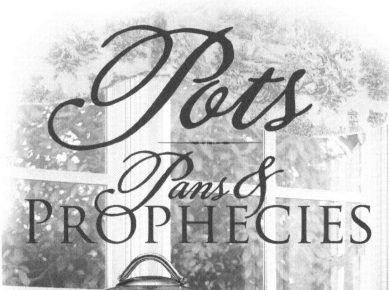

CONCLUSION

POTS, PANS & PROPHECIES
Conclusion

What a wonderful example of a vessel of
honor for God we have in Mary!

I have enjoyed looking at just a small portion of her life through the Word according to Luke's gospel. She was faithful to God and His will. As a result, we are blessed and so was she.

Mary loved Jesus both as her Son and as her Savior. She was the first to hold Him and minister to Him, but she also received from His ministry. She followed Him as a believer and knew Him as her Redeemer. She saw Him take His first step as a toddler and she saw Him perform His first miracle as the Messiah.

She believed His teachings and witnessed the power of His preaching firsthand. Yes, she was His mother, but more than that, she was His follower, a believer and a true disciple of Jesus Christ. She was the first to receive revelation knowledge of who He was.

And the greater the revelation the less the
reservation!

Mary stayed with Him until the very end, and then was present when "the end" became "the beginning" after the resurrection.

She was faithful to His commands and was one of the 120 in the upper room prayer meeting on the day of Pentecost and was a recipient of the outpouring of the Holy Spirit that came to those who tarried in obedience. She also reared her other children to believe and follow Jesus. (See Acts 1:14)

Yes, what an example of obedience Mary left for us!

We have determined as we studied together from *Pots, Pans & Prophecies* that we would be those vessels of honor for the Father's purpose in these last days. I feel it is fitting that we conclude our study by taking her instruction as our final thought.

Let's look to the Word again and read, and take what would still be her advice to us today as servants of Jesus Christ.

His mother said to the servants, Whatever He says to you, do *it* (John 2:5 AB).

And to that we say, "Amen!"

CONCLUSION

Other Products Available
from International Women's Discipleship

If you have been inspired by *Pots, Pans & Prophecies*, check out other Bible studies and products available from Women's Discipleship on our website **www. womendiscipleshipcog.com**.

Women's Discipleship
1.423.478.7286
www.womendiscipleioscog.com

Pots, Pans & Prophecies teaching DVD is to be used by the facilitator/leader in conjunction with the participant/leaders guide. It can be paused for participant questions and discussion. A local church study group may choose to let Rhonda "teach," or they can pick and choose what portions to play during the study. The DVD is a valuable resource.

ISBN: 978-1-940682-01-3

Pots, Pans & Prophecies Bible study and teaching DVD combo is to be used by a facilitator/leader or for personal Bible study.

ISBN: 978-1-940682--02-0

Coins, Covenant & Character is the second Bible study in the Kindle the Power discipleship series from International Women's Discipleship, written by Rhonda K. Holland.

The Great Physician is watching over you with an eternal, everlasting love. His love will light your way and restoration will be yours. He is pouring in the healing oil. You will find all you have lost. There is no condemnation for your past failures! You will find your Coins of Covenant have increased because you have been in the presence of the Great Physician: Your commitment to walk in covenant with Him will be stronger than ever.

ISBN: 978-1-59684-675-3

Monedas, Pacto y Carácter is the spanish version of the *Coins, Covenant and Character* Bible study in the Kindle the Power discipleship series from International Women's Discipleship written by Rhonda K. Holland.

El Médico Divino cuida de usted con amor eterno. Su amor alumbrará su camino hacia la restauración. No la abandonará durante el proceso de recuperación. Ahora mismo, está derramando sobre usted su aceite sanador. Usted se recuperará. Encontrará lo que ha perdido. ¡Nadie la condenará por sus fracasos! ¡Será recompensada por lo que ha sufrido en esta vida y nada la separará del amor de Dios! Verá un aumento en sus Monedas del Pacto porque estuvo en la presencia del Médico Divino: compasión, bondad, gentileza, mansedumbre, paciencia, perseverancia, perdón, amor, paz y gratitud. Su fuerza aumentará a medida que ande en pacto con Dios.

ISBN: 978-1-940682-03-7

Coins, Covenant & Character teaching DVD is to be used by the facilitator/leader in conjunction with the participant/leaders guide. The DVD can be paused for participant questions and discussion. A local church study group may choose to let Rhonda "teach" or they can pick and choose what portions of the DVD to play during the study.

ISBN: 978-1-59684-676-0

Giants, Grapes & Grasshoppers is the first Bible study in the *Kindle the Power* discipleship series from International Women's Discipleship.

Author and speaker, Rhonda K. Holland, helps participants discover who they are in Christ as they pull down strongholds through the power of fruitfulness and praise!

ISBN: 978-1-59684-624-1

Gigantes, Uvas y Langostas is the first Bible study in the *Kindle the Power* discipleship series from International Women's Discipleship.

Author and speaker, Rhonda K. Holland, helps participants discover who they are in Christ as they pull down strongholds through the power of fruitfulness and praise!

ISBN: 978-1-59684-715-6

Giants, Grapes & Grasshoppers teaching DVD is to be used by the facilitator/leader in conjunction with the participant/leaders guide.

ISBN: 978-1-59684-625-8

Kindle the Power Journal is a way to journal our faith journey and personal testimony, details of answered prayers, and the "aha" moments of insights gained in personal Bible study. Such a legacy of meaningful moments can be passed on to our children and grandchildren as a testimony of the *grace* of God.

ISBN: 978-1-59684-676-0

Pots, Pans & PROPHECIES

What Others are Saying

Giants, Grapes, & Grasshoppers is an amazing Bible Study packed full of the word. It shows you how to overcome the giants in your life through praise and to see yourself as God sees you—A Child of the King! As we focus on God and who He is, His peace will rule in our hearts and lives! So do you see the *Giants, Grapes, or Grasshoppers* in your situation? I now see the Grapes!

—*Samantha Chase, Artesia, New Mexico*

Our Sunday school class studied *Giants, Grapes and Grasshoppers* as well as *Coins, Covenant & Character*. We have seasoned believers and new converts and all were touched and challenged to grow in our Christian walk. We are really looking forward to the next study.

—*Brenda Roberts, Mesquite, Texas*

Giants, Grapes & Grasshoppers is one of the most uplifting and inspirational books I have ever read, written by the most anointed author and speaker I have ever been blessed to hear. Every line of every chapter is purposed by God.

—*Janet Whitmore, Anniston, Alabama*

I was delighted to be able to lead this study! It was a complete joy for me to see the women in my study begin to grasp who they are in Christ. So many women are conditioned to think of themselves as inferior. In *Giants, Grapes & Grasshoppers*, Rhonda shows us how to take our eyes off our circumstances and focus on God, trusting that He wants more for us than we can even imagine if only we can learn to trust Him enough to praise Him through every circumstance. We are not grasshoppers to be stepped on. Though hard pressed, we are not crushed. We are in a spiritual warfare but we can stand as giants, tall and mighty in the Spirit of the Lord!

—*Kathy Mooneyham Cook, Kennesaw, Georgia*

Giants, Grapes and Grasshoppers is insightful, inspiring, and down to earth. The content touches almost every aspect of every day living and if those studying this will apply the Word to their heart, it will be life changing. You cannot help but be refreshed after participating in this anointed teaching. It greatly impacted and changed my life. From the first chapter which taught us to be positive in our spirit to the foundation of 'praise' instead of 'worry' to 'cultivating' good thoughts and throwing out the bad thoughts which bring 'peace' to our hearts. And then 'powerful praise' leads us to knowing who we are in Christ and being able to have the victory over the devil. This is powerful teaching and is needed for all Christians!

—*Gail Gore, Fayetteville, North Carolina*

Pots, Pans & PROPHECIES

My "giant" was breast cancer. I guess the worst thing about fighting cancer is the fear that it will come back. God has been so faithful, and He carried me through that fire. But, I kept thinking "Ok, I'm still young and I will probably go through more fires. Will they be worse than cancer? Will He walk me through those as well?" I think it was the second week of the study when Rhonda used Hebrews 13:5 (AMP)—"for He [God] Himself has said, I will not in any way fail you nor give you up nor leave you without support. [I will} not, [I will} not, [I will] not in any degree leave you helpless nor forsake nor let [you] down (relax my hold on you)!" I have heard and read this verse all my life, but I guess I never really let it sink in. He said He won't relax His hold on me! Those were the absolute most comforting words I have ever heard, and the Holy Spirit just wrapped His arms around me and confirmed in me that His word is faithful and true. What a beautiful promise!

—*Susie Sluka, Covington, Washington*

Pots, Pans & PROPHECIES

Pots, Pans & PROPHECIES

About the Author

Rhonda K. Holland is a women's conference and retreat speaker, minister and teacher of the Word. She and her husband, Kenneth, have two adult sons, Joel and Jonathan. Rhonda is on staff at the South Aiken Church of God in South Carolina, where she and her family are involved in various areas of ministry. She has a passion and desire to minister to the body of Christ in these last days. Her heart for God and her love for the Word are felt as she ministers to those hurting and hungry for His presence.

Pots, Pans & PROPHECIES

Made in the USA
Columbia, SC
01 February 2020